Of Borders and Dreams
A Mexican-American Experience
of Urban Education

Of Borders and Dreams
A Mexican-American Experience of Urban Education

WITHDRAWN

Chris Liska Carger

TEACHERS
COLLEGE
PRESS

Teachers College, Columbia University
New York and London

371.976872
C2760
1996

Published by Teachers College Press, 1234 Amsterdam Avenue, New York, NY 10027

Library of Congress Cataloging-in-Publication Data

Carger, Chris Liska.
    Of borders and dreams : a Mexican-American experience of urban
education / by Chris Liska Carger.
        p.   cm.
    Includes bibliographical references and index.
    ISBN 0-8077-3523-X (alk. paper). — ISBN 0-8077-3522-1 (pbk. :
alk. paper)
    1. Mexican-American children—Education (Elementary)—Illinois—
Chicago—Case studies.   2. Education, Urban—Illinois—Chicago—
Case studies.   I. Title.
    LC2688.C54C37   1996/
    371.97'6872'077311—dc20   95-26206

ISBN 0-8077-3522-1 (paper)
ISBN 0-8077-3523-X (cloth)

Printed on acid-free paper

Manufactured in the United States of America

03 02 01 00 99 98 97   8 7 6 5 4 3 2

This book is dedicated to the Juarez family, whose faith and perseverance inspired me, and to Jim, Elizabeth, and Mary Carger, who offered constant support as they crossed borders of their own while a wife and mother wrote of the struggles another family faced.

All names, locations, and identifying details have been changed in order to protect the anonymity of the people in this narrative.

Contents

Foreword

Every Alejandro Juarez in the world deserves to find his Chris Carger. Alejandro is the central figure in the story you are about to read; Carger is the dazzling writer of that story, Alejandro's gifted biographer. She was once his teacher, a very special teacher who looked beyond the labels and stereotypes heaped high upon him by well-meaning but misguided school people; she saw the heart of the child. During his early adolescence she was his tutor, his *maestra*, his interpreter, his advocate. And at some point she became, as well, his chronicler, his observer, and his recorder. Through it all she managed, somehow, to resist the role of the distant pedagogue or the bloodless researcher, refused to check her commitments and her passions at the door of the system or the academy, and she remained in the deepest sense his friend and compañera. Their relationship was fully human—heart to heart, hand to hand, head to head. What she accomplishes here is a portrait that laughs and aches and shouts—a detailed account of growing up poor and Mexican in a crowded barrio on the margins of one of the most splendid cities in the richest country in the world. It is a story of contrasts and contradictions as well as connection, of borders and boundaries, but also of bridges.

Chris Carger's portrait of Alejandro reminds us that all children bring capacity with them to school, that every child is a three-dimensional being like ourselves with hopes, dreams, skills, knowledge, and spirit. It is an antidote to the common caricature of poor, immigrant, or city kids as all deficit, all danger, all difficulty. Seeing Alejandro as whole, as a person of thought and feeling, as a growing, striving individual, points toward a reasonable starting point for an education of purpose for him, even as it helps us see the problems built deeply into the social structures, the institutions, the schools we have created. For the truth is that most schools most of the time (and overwhelmingly in poor city schools) are incapable of focusing on capacity—they tend, rather, to reduce individuals to anonymous bits of the crowd, to hammer senselessly at perceived weaknesses and, in the process, to turn teachers into clerks and students into problems, encumbrances, obstacles. Kids become known, then, by their deficits, and teachers find it tough to understand, access, or to even see the capacity that is certainly there.

Focusing on Alejandro does not cut Carger off from the contexts of his being—the concentric circles of family, language, cultural web, historical flow, and economic condition. Carger reminds us that to be child-centered is necessarily to be family-centered, for children are nested in families and to be for the child must mean to be for the family. To begin to really understand the difficulties and problems Alejandro faces, one must also see the pressures the family endures. Alma, his mother, and Alejandro, Sr., his father, become transcendent figures here, steady, hard-working, everyday heroes. After a string of setbacks and defeats in their fight for their son's education, Alma says to Chris, "When you have your children . . . everything is happiness. . . . My husband and I were so thrilled with our babies. We never thought about the problems that could happen later on." We are ready to cry, and we fully expect her to give up because that is exactly what we would do at this point. The pain is too great, the pressure to present herself and her family as pathological in order to access the most meager resources is too demanding. But she is back with a plan and a strategy the next day: "I think this will work, Chris," she says hopefully, and in that simple affirmation she renews our faith in the deep well of possibility in the human spirit.

The dominant theme in this book is of crossing borders, the Rio Grande in the beginning, but, later on, the boundaries of ignorance, the borders of literacy, the frontiers of full participation. It is about walls erected between reasonable dreams and unreasonable worlds, and the struggle to breach those barricades. Most important, it is about Chris Carger's own effort to push the limit of what counts in teaching and in research, to break from the limits of "service" and to meet Alejandro instead in authentic human solidarity. Because this is the story of a life being lived, it is necessarily dynamic, vivid, rough; because it is an American tale, oppression goes hand in hand with hope, cruelty with kindness, discrimination with determination. Finally, there are no smooth edges here, no easy answers, no happy endings. Far from a weakness, this is Carger's singular achievement.

—William Ayers

Acknowledgments

I would like to thank Bill Ayers, Bill Schubert, and Ann Lopez Schubert for their indefatigable encouragement in my writing of this book, their belief in narrative, and their commitment to meaningful and sensitive curriculum for all children. I also want to acknowledge the support and patient advice of Sister Faith in reviewing my narrative and listening, with heart, to my concerns for Alejandro. I would like to express my gratitude to the writers I read—Sandra Cisneros, Carmen Tafolla, Luis Rodriguez, Victor Villaseñor, Nash Candelaria, Gloria Anzaldúa, and Julia Alvarez—for so eloquently voicing the poetry and stories of their immigrant and minority journeys in this country, inspiring me to tell of yet another's experience. My sincere gratitude is extended as well to Alex Kotlowitz, who, through his own writing, showed me how to tell such a story as a participant observer, resource, and friend who was crossing cultural borders. Mere words cannot convey my appreciation to Alma and Alejandro Juarez for their willingness to open borders and share their lives, their dreams, and their family stories with me. Finally, unending thanks to my husband. Without his long hours at the computer and tireless discussions of my work, this book would not have materialized.

Of Borders and Dreams: Beginnings

. . . Kino's face was set, and his mind and his will were set. "This is our one chance," he said. "Our son must go to school. He must break out of the pot that holds us in."

—*The Pearl*, J. Steinbeck

"*Maestra* [teacher], what do you think about us moving out of the neighborhood and away from Sorrowful Mother School? My sister wants us to move to a little house, the apartment below hers. She says the public schools there are good. I just don't know what to do."

Two years before this phone call, I met Alma Juarez at the front door of her apartment on the west side of Chicago. The predominantly Mexican area where she lived is an aging urban nest of small brick homes, run-down shops, and littered streets. The silver mirror-like windows of the Cook County jail complex loom above the entire neighborhood, an eerie reminder of danger and pain. Alleys, garages, school and store walls are coated with gang graffiti. The long-eared rabbit of the Latin Kings, a gang active on Chicago's west side, is a familiar picture to the hundreds of Mexican-American children for whom this barrio is home. Yet despite its problems, the area is alive with Latino families; the streets and shops bustle with activity. People sell from shops, store fronts, and the backs of trucks, and everywhere there are children.

Alma's apartment was next to an abandoned wooden house where local gang kids and addicts took refuge. She and her husband never allowed their five children to play outside. Alejandro, Ricardo, Alicia, Almita, and Lupita were sequestered in their second floor home day in and day out, like precious little birds in a cage surrounded by hungry cats.

Alejandro, their oldest child, in fifth grade then, had been referred to Sorrowful Mother's English as a Second Language (ESL) program, which I coordinated under the auspices of a local college. That year I

1

could not find a tutor for the middle grade ESL groups, which met in the afternoon, so I decided to teach the groups myself. And that is how I found Alejandro Juarez. He walked hesitantly into the spacious, old, high ceilinged room we used for ESL classes along with John, his classmate newly arrived from Poland. They stood together, in stark contrast. Alejandro, a handsome boy with tan skin, shiny dark hair, and doe-like deep brown eyes, stood before me. His stance was tentative; he looked at the floor. John, fair-skinned, blond-haired, and blue-eyed, confidently strolled into the room and in halting English engaged me in conversation immediately. As the three of us worked in one small corner of the large classroom each Tuesday and Thursday afternoon, we somehow knitted together our very different life experiences as we struggled with the teaching and learning of a new language and literacy. As I worked with Alejandro each week I saw that his needs went beyond those of a second language learner. John quickly surpassed him in reading, although John had been in this country a much shorter time. I began to use some of the strategies I knew for learning disabled readers with Alejandro but saw little progress in his struggle with print. His memory for letters, sounds, and words, in both English and Spanish, seemed incredibly weak. Yet, he tried so hard to succeed.

So that summer, I called his mother, introduced myself as her son's ESL teacher, and asked if I could take Alejandro to the college's Diagnostic Center to look into his textual literacy problems more thoroughly. She agreed to send him but only if she could accompany us.

"I'm sorry to tag along, *Maestra*. But I don't really know you."

I understood perfectly; Alejandro was her son and literally meant the world to her. I was a stranger on the other end of a phone line speaking Anglicized Spanish.

As we crossed from the city's west side to the more affluent north, Alma poured out her heart to me regarding her son's academic problems. She spoke of her and her husband's own minimal literacy in Spanish and English. She told of her frustration in having to find cousins, friends, or neighbors to accompany her to the doctor's office, the bank, the pharmacy because she needed help to read and write.

"I just don't want Alejandro to have to go through what I do, *Maestra*. I always have to drag someone along with me for help. I just want him to be able to read."

A simple dream for many, but not for Alma and her children. They had no one to help them with homework or read them a story. Even a note home about a school event was a struggle for this family.

So Alma spent the day waiting for her son to be tested, even though she worked the night before and hadn't slept. She brought tapes to listen to and a lunch for Alejandro that could have fed two children, maybe three. I admired her. What she could not do for her son academically, she did superbly in her attention to his physical needs. All of her five children were immaculately groomed and dressed, lovingly cared for according to her own strengths.

By the next day, Alma trusted me enough to take her son alone to the college to finish his evaluation. Throughout the next 2 years as Alejandro continued in the ESL program we became friends. She periodically called me by phone, sent little gifts at the holidays, always offering to cook dinner for me and my family some day. And so, the phone call about the difficult decision to move arrived last summer. Alejandro would soon be in eighth grade.

I encouraged Alma to move her family to a safer neighborhood. She did. They now live on a clean, tree-lined street full of well-kept homes in a neighborhood with Polish and Mexican families. The children can play outside and ride their bikes to a nearby park. There are neighbors next door instead of abandoned buildings. But the move did not bring everything Alma and her husband had hoped for.

I accompanied Alma, Alejandro, and Alma's four younger children, Alicia, Lupita, Almita, and Ricardo to Shepherd School, the public school in their new neighborhood. She had called the school months before making the decision to move and was told that her children would be accepted as long as she could prove residency in the school's enrollment area. Yet the day she asked me to come with her, there were problems. Only her four younger children were accepted into the school despite Alma's pleas to take all five.

"I'm sure you know what a controlled enrollment means," snapped the school principal. "We're an overcrowded school; I can't fit one more eighth grader in the class. Absolutely not."

"But his four siblings have been accepted here; isn't it the policy to keep a family together?" I questioned.

"Look, you can tell her [pointing to Alma] that I don't have to take *any* of her children. If she wants to put four here and have the oldest bused to another school, she can. Or she can have all five bused. I don't care. I don't have to take any of them."

"Is there a waiting list for the eighth grade?" I persisted, "and do you have an English as a Second Language program and a remedial reading program? I have questions I'd like to ask you about the programs available in these schools."

"Look, you could do this with a phone call, or a letter, or you could come back another day. This could be just a letter. Just put it in a letter," the principal impatiently replied.

I went out to the hallway with Alma, translated the principal's message, feeling upset and incredulous at its blunt delivery. Alma and I began the process of registering the four younger children and as we did I told the secretary how terribly disappointed we were with the situation.

"This is a sweet, close-knit family," I told her. "Alejandro is very much the big brother who watches over his younger brother and sisters. I can't tell you how disappointed I am in this situation. When Mrs. Juarez called in June she was told nothing of overcrowding problems." After hearing the plight of the overcrowded school in more civil tones from the secretary and how the school board's deal to buy an extra building fell through during the summer, I asked her what she thought of the school Alejandro would be bused to if Mrs. Juarez registered him as well.

"Well, I'm telling you this as a parent now, not as a school employee. I live in this neighborhood, too. I'd be very upset. That school is riddled with gangs. They'd eat him alive."

"Where is it?" I asked.

"Well, it's actually in the neighborhood they moved out of," she laughed. "He's a handsome boy; they'll be after him. Tell her [pointing to Alma] she should scar his face or something so he doesn't look so cute [she joked]. Seriously, he needs to keep his nose clean and not get involved right from the start. There are gangs here too; they're everywhere, but it's a little better here. I'll tell you, though, I used to live in the area where they're busing and I left to get away from *those* gangs."

Alma understood none of this conversation in English. As we walked out of the school I said, "Alma, you can't send him to that other school. It's full of gangs; they'll hurt him. The secretary said it's very dangerous. Can you afford to put him back at the parochial school in your old neighborhood for one more year?" As we walked through the alley to their new home, tears rolled down her cheeks, the first time I had ever seen something rattle Alma.

"My relatives told my husband it's the same in Mexico. He says he wants to sell our home in Mexico and buy one near your house some day, *Maestra*. He says you'll help us protect Alejandro from the gangs." Tears stained her cheeks again. Alejandro looked at his mother silently, fear filling his deep brown eyes.

Alma held on to the kernel of hope tossed to us by the sympathetic secretary. She had suggested that we wait a day to enroll Alejandro in the other school.

"We'll call Mrs. Juarez tomorrow in case we get an opening," said the secretary. "They'll look at his name and because he has four broth-

ers and sisters here, he'd be one of the first to get taken in. I'll definitely call her tomorrow." Alma stopped crying and remembered the
secretary's promise.

"Maybe tomorrow, maybe tomorrow they'll take him." It was the
first of many times I would witness Alma's indefatigable resilience.

Later that night, as I recounted the bitterly ironic story to my
husband, I cried for Alma. "They want to bus her son back to the neighborhood she tried to leave behind," I told him. Alma's predicament
made me think of Steinbeck's novel, *The Pearl* (1947). I thought of
Alma and her husband's attempt to make it out of the poverty and
danger of their old neighborhood just as Kino and Juana tried to make
it out of the poverty of their village. I remembered the neighbors in
Steinbeck's novel thinking, ". . . God punished Kino because he re-
belled against the way things are" (p. 39).

"My son will read and open the books, and my son will write and
know writing . . . and these things will make us free because he will
know—he will know and through him we will know. . . . This is what
the pearl will do," prophesied Kino in Steinbeck's work (1947, p. 38).
Alma's confession that she always had to drag someone along to read
for her, echoed in my mind as did Kino's hope that his son would learn
to read and finally, "one of his own people could tell him the truth of
things" (p. 52). The Juarezes' dream of literacy for their son, 50 years
later in an urban "village," was the same as Kino's. Reasonable dreams
in an unreasonable world.

I also recalled, in *The Pearl*, the callous doctor's refusal to help the
baby Coyotito when he was bitten by a scorpion. "'I am a doctor, not
a veterinarian,' he said in contempt of the Indian child" (p. 18).

"I don't have to take any of her children," the principal said, in
contempt of the Mexican students. The poison of the principal's apathy
seemed as potent to me as the scorpion's. Alma and her husband hold
the pearl of education for their children so tenaciously in their palms.
They have not yet tossed it back into the sea. I hoped that the parallels
would end here, for the end of *The Pearl* is so brutally hopeless.

"My father's gonna take me to see my cousin's face; it's all beat
up from the gangs," Alejandro said softly as we walked back from the
school that refused to take him.

"My husband wants him to see what can happen when you hang
out with the gangs," explained Alma.

"How would you feel about going back to the Sorrowful Mother,
Alejandro?" I asked.

"I want to go back," he said anxiously. "Here I'm afraid; there it
will be better." For the first time that afternoon he smiled.

Alejandro called me the next evening. The school secretary never contacted them as promised. To return to his old school, Alejandro now awakens at 4:00 a.m. so his father can drop him off at his *comadre's* [godmother's] apartment in the same building they thought they had left behind. There Alejandro waits from 5:00 until 8:00 when school begins at Sorrowful Mother, where he re-enrolled. After school he waits again until 4 p.m., when his father picks him up after work. His evenings are spent cleaning their new apartment and struggling through incomprehensible homework and written punishments for low test scores in a class with a teacher unprepared to teach a limited-English-proficient student with learning problems. He has failed in almost every course he's taken so far this year.

"Right, teachers aren't supposed to shove you?" Alejandro asked me and recounted stories of his disgruntled eighth-grade teacher. "She makes fun of the kids who can't speak English, tells them they're going to end up working in McDonalds all their life. She shouldn't do that, right?"

"I don't like what his teacher does but at least he's safe from the gangs," lamented his father.

"*Tenía tantas ilusiones,*" said Alma, wistfully, of her husband. "He had so many dreams for his son."

In the 20 years I have taught Latino children both in New York and Chicago, I have seen the plight of families like Alejandro's searching for an appropriate education for their sons and daughters over and over again. I have heard of this "population" referred to as "a problem," and in the middle of my fortieth year, as a doctoral student embarking upon a dissertational journey, that "problem" landed squarely in my path once again. For my dissertation, I had planned, at one point, to study the effects of using multicultural children's literature to teach English as a Second Language to Latino kindergartners. At another juncture, I had chosen to examine the school lives of three middle-grade Mexican students who had attended ESL classes. I had even started to collect data, interviewing the families of two such students in a predominantly Mexican community on the southwest side of Chicago. But Alejandro, the most complicated case to study, was clearly the most compelling choice of the three possibilities. Something drew me to this child and his family like a moth to a flame and I headed straight for the light. I set aside the other studies. It was not the first time, in my career as a teacher, nor do I think it will be the last, that I felt compelled to become involved with a certain student. It is not their neediness that compels me, although in various forms it is often present. For just as present there exists a lovely giftedness of one

sort or another that they have to offer. It is something deep and recip-
rocal, whatever it is. Gary Paulsen, an author I admire who writes about
the wilderness, animals, and, in one book, a Native American, used the
word *mind-touch* to describe the unspoken profound form of communication one character felt from another. "And yet there was that thing,
that strange feeling, or look, or smell, or mind-touch that passed between them. And when it was done they knew each other in a way that
few people ever know each other" (Paulsen, 1978, p. 83). That is something of what I felt between myself and Alejandro and his family. I would
call it a "heart-touch." So I abandoned the data I had compiled and
began to focus on Alejandro. I refused to call him the subject of my
study and only with sarcasm described the mandatory "problem" with
which I grappled, defying the traditional dissertation format. The
"problem," I wrote,

> a child born in this country to Mexican parents, who have
> clawed their way out of abject poverty; whose native language is
> Spanish; who, despite textual illiteracy and racism, tenaciously
> hold on to deep religious convictions and cultural values; whose
> lives center around their family and dreams of a better life for
> their cherished first-born child, all of their children, *llena de
> ilusions* [full of hopes] . . . truly is not the problem. The prob-
> lem . . . is educational systems which have not adapted success-
> fully to such diversity, which have not looked into the face of
> such a child and seen beauty and potential, but function instead
> in a deficit finding mode. Systems that have not accepted varied
> ways of talking, knowing, doing, and valuing . . . nor offered a
> helping hand to cross the borders life presents to such students,
> that frequently cannot even offer a safe environment in which to
> attempt to educate such a child. The problem . . . the education
> of the Alejandros of this country . . . begs resolution.

By the year 2000, the U.S. Census Bureau data conservatively
projects a school-aged population of about 3.5 million limited-English-
proficient students, not counting the children of undocumented workers. Presently, about 80% of that student population are Spanish-speaking with Mexican backgrounds, the most predominant of the five major
Latino groups (Mexican 13.3 million, Central American 2.6 million,
Puerto Rican 2.2 million, Cuban 1 million, Caribbean 1.4 million)
(Augenbraum & Stavans, 1993). In addition, population trends indi-
cate that the Hispanic population has the most rapid increase relative to
that of other minorities and to the overall population of the United States

(Trueba, 1989). It appears that Hispanics will continue to dominate the rolls of the limited-English-proficient in classrooms of the twenty-first century. Hispanics also suffer the highest dropout rate in the country, reported at 40% nationally by age 14 (Duran, 1983; Walker, 1987). A 70% dropout rate for Hispanic high school students is reported in the city of Chicago (Perez-Miller, 1991). Consistent with these figures are the very low numbers of Hispanic students who pursue college careers, particularly in the areas of math and science (Walker, 1987).

Alejandro was, I feared, on the road to becoming part of the chilling statistics on Latino dropouts in the city of Chicago. He was a student embodying many characteristics seen as challenging to educators: urban Mexican-American background, of low and threatened economic income, having very little parental schooling or literacy at home, bilingual yet not possessing a strongly developed first or second language, having special learning needs and significant memory and literacy difficulties. Born in Chicago, he attended kindergarten at the local Chicago public school near his apartment, then moved to Mexico where he attended part of first grade and all of second grade in a parochial school where classes were conducted in Spanish. He and his family eventually returned to Chicago where he returned to another public school for third grade, then transferred to a Chicago parochial school for fourth through eighth grade during which he was immersed in English.

The result of Alejandro's educational journey thus far was total confusion between the phonetic systems of English and Spanish, greatly affecting his ability to read and write. Compounding his problem with literacy is his parents' inability to provide him with experiences with the printed word. Although they give Alejandro an incredibly strong family network and a warm, loving environment in which to grow, they are not textually literate in Spanish or English and were not able to read to him as a child or help with homework over the years. A simple daily event like receiving mail, taken for granted as a routine occasion for literacy by many, is a struggle in Alejandro's family. He is relied on to decipher what arrives at home, but he still lacks the decoding skills to comprehend accurately.

One day while visiting his home I watched him try to figure out a sales promotion that arrived through the mail from a department store chain. His four siblings crowded around him at the kitchen table with anxious faces as he looked with confusion at the packet of information addressed to his father. "My Dad told me to look at this for him," he said.

"They're just trying to sell jewelry," I explained to him as he looked at the small booklet filled with watches, necklaces, and rings.

"Oh, they want my father to sell jewelry!" he responded.

"No," I said, "they want him to *buy* the jewelry." I then showed Alejandro and his brother and sisters how the letters next to the jewelry pieces had matching lettered paragraphs on the bottom of the page describing the pieces and their prices.

"Ohhh!" they sighed, excitedly buzzing about jewelry they liked and looking for the prices as if the directions for a new game had finally "rung a bell."

I wondered how they are able to make sense of other mail—bills, forms, and correspondence from schools—and function in their world. I wondered how Alejandro was able to face the world of his eighth-grade classes each day not feeling hopelessly submerged by the print he encounters so unsuccessfully there as well. On his last two report cards, he failed every subject except physical education.

What brought me to this problem, to this study and the tremendous compassion I feel for Alejandro whose story I have chosen to voice? What touched my heart?

I was the daughter of blue-collar workers whose bigotry was blatant at times, ambivalent at others, banished at moments. I grew up during the swirl of ideas and idealism that was the 1960s. I had a mother whose vague dissatisfaction with her life permeated all she did but who, with support and direction from caring Catholic school teachers, had the ability to spark in me the value of creativity and the appreciation of cultural diversity. Both of my parents centered much of their lives around their daughters' education. Unknowingly, they breathed life into my curriculum. People with little formal education—one with only an elementary school diploma, one with high school—they pursued and valued the ideas I brought home. When I studied non-Western culture, Chinese lanterns and dolls appeared on our living room shelves; when I read the *Quijote* as a Spanish major in college, a print of Picasso's beleaguered knight was hung on our living room wall; and as I struggled to become proficient in Spanish as my second language, the money was scraped together by my mother to fly me to my Cuban girlfriend's summer home in Puerto Rico. That $40 ticket helped to set in motion what would become for me a lifelong association with Latino cultures. Although my mother's bitterness toward what life had or had not dealt her would make our relationship more and more difficult as my education blossomed, I cannot thank her enough for what she tried to do for me. She brought curriculum to life; it lifted my life to new heights. My father, a quiet, talented man who spent his life working on a factory assembly line, affirmed his respect for the education I pursued so successfully, by enrolling in night school, in his mid-fifties, to surprise me with earning a GED diploma while I was away at college. My pride in his accomplishment is unspeakable.

So now I was looking at the life of a young man whose parents had even less schooling than mine, but the same focus on and belief in the importance of education for their children. They, too, encourage the English language for their children, with the same belief that my parents had in the increased employment opportunities it might some-day offer. Their religious beliefs and economic level are quite compa-rable as well. Where the similarities sharply end is in the areas of lan-guage and literacy and racism. My father gave up his home language to become fluent in English. In fact, I never knew he could speak Pol-ish until my graduate school years when I brought home for dinner a Polish second language student whom I was tutoring. To my surprise, he and my father struck up a conversation in their native language. My maternal grandfather, who had a pronounced French accent and al-ways switched into his native tongue when any emotional moment arose, never taught my mother a word of French. Both of my parents were textually literate and competent in the mainstream language of the country where they lived, although their grasp of grammar was never quite standard. Neither of my parents suffered the scourges of racism as they and their parents blended into the melting pot that was their national experience. Religious discrimination as Catholics in a very Protestant community was the only form of intolerance they experi-enced, and I as their daughter saw its consequences unfold but would leave it behind once I went away to college.

In contrast, Alejandro's parents have maintained their native tongue and passed it on to their children, although they never fully attained lit-eracy in it, having received no more than a second-grade formal educa-tion. Alma and her husband, Alejandro, Sr., can live their whole lives in Chicago *barrios* speaking Spanish, taking care of business in local shops, attending Spanish masses at church. They struggle greatly with oral English and have no second language literacy, although they have learned enough receptive English to survive in low paying, unskilled jobs. Alma once joked with me about her problems with English, saying someone would have to find a way to enter into her brain and clean it thoroughly for her ever to hope to learn *inglés* [English]. They have passed on a rich cultural milieu in which they and their children live their lives, yet their problems with English plague them and their children outside of their family context and Latino neighborhoods. Alejandro's mother recounted bitterly, yet with a tone of resignation, the harassment she suffered from a white manager who treated the Mexican women in her factory miser-ably as compared with white fellow workers.

"Me habla muy feo" ["he speaks to me in an ugly way"], she lamented. Often she feels that her input is not valued or acknowledged although she has good ideas to offer on the organization of their work duties. She was spoken to with a total lack of respect. She was given the most grueling work to do and frequently could not use her hands fully because of 10 hours spent pounding cartons closed on her "line." She coughed deeply from the tiny particles of paper she inhaled day in and day out in the cardboard carton factory where she and her three sisters work. "I don't want Alejandro to have to put up with what I do in my job," she said emphatically.

Alejandro, Sr., in a quieter manner, attested to the hindrance his lack of English skills presented him at work: "I tell Alejandro that we want him to take advantage of an education and learn English now. Because once he starts working, opportunities will pass him by if he can't fill out forms in English and speak up for himself." He worked two jobs a day, with about 4 hours left to sleep, to support his family. The threat of returned unemployment always hovered over their household; they have lived through it before. "My son asks me why I do it," he continued, "why I work so many hours at two jobs. I tell him, you do what you have to do."

The Juarez family, which reflects the bronzed race that is *Aztlan* (descendants of Aztecs), has experienced persistent and abiding prejudice from employers, educators, and community members in general. Alejandro recounted his amazement and fear when, at his father's suggestion, he stopped in a small local grocery store for some cookies on a day when he had no time for breakfast before school. When he came to the register to pay, he was made to open his backpack and have it searched by the owner, who suspected him of shoplifting. His mother relates the story and how Alejandro then said he won't stop to buy cookies any more, even if his dad gives him the money, and even if he has to go to school hungry. They had not melted into that infamous American pot. Their story, their sincerity, their struggle touch me.

As I came to know the family, I began to hear the rich narratives of Alejandro's mother. I learned of their journey north, their dreams and disappointments, their incredible ability to persevere. I watched their fragile yet resilient hope to build a safe home and find something their eldest son could do with his life, as it became battered by the storms of urban life for an immigrant family. I saw, in particular, their experience of American education, their consistent marginalization in that system. I watched them cross borders and relinquish dreams, yet somehow hold on to hope, to the elusive and emancipating pearl of education. And I crossed borders of my own in the process.

Borders

It was a metaphor to fill our lives—that river, that first crossing, the mother of all crossings.

—*Always Running*, L. Rodriguez

For almost a full year I had been working closely with Alejandro, observing him and visiting his family. Once or twice during that time Alma had alluded to her initial crossing into the United States. She had mentioned that someday she'd like to tell me the whole story. On a beautiful, sunny summer afternoon that day finally came.

I asked Alma if I could sit and talk with her about the town she and her husband were born in and where Alejandro had attended first and second grades. It was called Juan de Carreo, she told me, in the Mexican state of Michoacán.

"And didn't you mention something about running away from the border patrol when you left Mexico?" I asked. "Can you tell me about your crossing into this country?" She grinned, and her story began.

"When we crossed *la frontera* [the border]? With a *coyote* [smuggler]?" she smiled and her deep brown eyes danced.

"I know that word—*coyote*," I told her. "I watched a movie once called 'El Norte' about a brother and sister from Central America who hired a *coyote* to get them across the Mexican border. He had them go through wide, rat infested pipes that ran across the border; it was terrible. The girl ended up getting a fever and dying a year later, but it was from the rat bites she got in that pipe." Alma just smiled, again.

"Oh, Tijuana is a miserable place, full of rats," Alma asserted.

"And one *coyote* these people in the movie hired actually robbed them; they're terrible to people, aren't they?" I asked.

"Let me tell you about the first time I tried to cross," answered Alma with a mischievous grin on her face. Little did I know that the story of "El Norte" paled in comparison to Alma's history at the border.

12

"It was my honeymoon," Alma began her story at the kitchen table. "We had been married for only 4 days. We hired a *coyote* to get us across the border." Alma was only 16 years old then. The economy of their small town in central Mexico, called the heartland, was so bad that they couldn't earn enough to survive. Alejandro Sr. had given his bride a choice of emigrating to Mexico City or trying to cross the border to California to try to make a better life together than they could have scratched out in Juan de Carreo. Alma chose the United States.

"The *coyote* had us in a taxi in Tijuana," she told me. "All of a sudden he told us to run out of the taxi. He saw immigration agents, he said. We didn't know any better so we ran and he rode away with everything we had—our money, our suitcases, all our clothes."

They didn't turn back, though, and tried to make the crossing at the river without the *coyote's* help but the water was too high that day. Alejandro had to grab Alma by the hand because she was being pulled away by the river, which, she explained, was very erratic due to dams she had heard about that were opened and closed at various times.

"*La Inmigración* [Immigration] put us on a bus to take us back to the other side," she remembered. "My husband was so nervous, he told me not to fall asleep on the bus. But Christina, I had gone 4 days without food and I couldn't stay awake. I had swallowed a lot of water in that river and it had made me sick so I had a fever too."

The river of which Alma spoke, I have since learned, is the Tía Juana River. It has a system of earthen dikes that retards its flow on the U.S. side but can cause backups and floods on the Mexican side. Mexico also pumps sewage into the river from its side of Tiajuana, which sextupled in size between 1950 and 1970, then doubled again in the 1980s (Weisman & Dusard, 1986). That was what made Alma so sick.

At one point later in her story she looked quizzically at her husband and said, "What *do* they call that river?"

"Uh, the Juarez, no, el Río Bravo, I think," he answered. She wasn't sure. Neither was he. Actually, Alma had crossed two different rivers during her border escapes, the Tía Juana and later, further to the east, the Río Grande, called the Río Bravo by Mexicans. I was struck by this lack of what I thought would have been geographic general knowledge. But later I realized that for Alma and Alejandro "that river" needed no special name; it was the only river of any importance in their lives; it was simply "*that* river": the one that separated their people from promises of prosperity and hope for survival, in a country where jobs cannot keep up with an expanding labor force.

Mexico has almost four times as many people as it did in 1940, and nearly three-quarters of the population is under the age of 30. It has been called an old country full of young people (Horan & Thompson, 1985). Since 1950 there has been a dramatic shift from rural, agriculturally based villages to urban, industrialized areas as country folk flock to cities in search of jobs (Horan & Thompson, 1985). Due only to an "accident of birth" that places some on the south side of a long, winding river, they earn vassal wages of 2½ cents per pound for picking vegetables from the same American corporations that pay farm workers in Texas or California about 8–9 cents a pound.

This was the plight of Alma and Alejandro, that of *campesinos* [farm workers] who could not feed their families. She sold fruit and vegetables at her father's small kiosk in their village in Michoacán, and Alejandro worked for years cleaning on a pig farm.

"His childhood was very tough and sad," Alma told me. There simply was not enough food, clothing, nothing for him and his nine brothers and sisters. At his own son Alejandro, Jr.'s age, 13, he had already left home to work.

"I think this is why my husband is so serious and works so hard, day and night," says Alma. "He doesn't want his children to go through what he did. He just had nothing. He hates to have to deny his own children anything."

"Well, I did fall asleep on that bus ride back into Mexico," recounted Alma, "and the driver had to slam on his brakes at one point and I rolled right onto the floor." The bus run by the border patrol was jam-packed, she explained. People were falling all around her. "My husband got so mad at me. I think it was because I was so young and he was so worried."

At various points during her story she would remind me jokingly, "and remember, this was my honeymoon!"

Alma and Alejandro tried to cross the border again the very next day. "It took us three tries within 4 days; we just kept trying again and again," she remembered. As she wove her story, she prepared dinner in her kitchen and seemed to enjoy retelling the drama she had experienced.

On their second attempt, Alma and Alejandro made it through the river and then had to scale a barbed wire fence. Her clothes got stuck on it, and Alejandro got upset and yelled at her as the border patrol chased them. He felt bad once Alma made it over and told her, "We can just go back to Mexico and forget this." "*Yo era muy necia*" ["I was very stupid"], said Alma. I said, "No, let's continue. God will help us."

Once they got through the fence there was a host of *coyotes* luring the frightened wetbacks into the woods. "There were many young women, many pregnant," explained Alma. "The *coyotes* were taking

women into the woods and raping them," she lowered her voice as one
of her children walked by. Alejandro and Alma ran and ran all night
long over the hills, to get away from them. Alma remembered her
husband telling her that it would be better to get caught by immigration than to have her taken by the *coyotes*. Early in the morning, when
they were almost across "the line," they were, in fact, caught by immigration for the second time.

Alma remembered the border patrolman saying in faltering Spanish, "*Hombres parados, mujeres sentados!*" ["Men stand, women sit!"]
to the little group of migrants he apprehended. She laughed. "Christina, I had a big smile on my face. I couldn't help it. It was the first
time I ever heard Spanish spoken like that and it just struck me so funny.
Oh, my husband was so aggravated with me!" I had seen Alma's incredible ability to see the humorous, even in the worst of situations,
throughout the year I had known her. I could imagine her at 16, hearing Anglicized Spanish for the first time, and catching the comedy of
it despite their failed crossing.

"These patrolmen were nasty," Alma remembered. "Alejandro and
I decided to give false names; I don't know why. We were just so scared.
This time we were put in jail for the day." Alicia, her 10-year-old daughter, overheard her and said, "Ma, jail? Why didn't you ever tell us all of
this?" "Well," Alma smiled and looked at me. She just sighed and continued her story.

The guards seemed to take a disliking to Alejandro, she remembered, and at one point slammed his fingers in the doorway. They separated some of the men, including Alejandro, from the rest of the group
and were going to drive them further into the countryside.

"They do this so that it will take them longer to get back to the
border and try to cross again," explained Alma. "I just cried and cried
and begged them not to take him. I told them he was my husband but
we had given different names and they didn't believe me at first."

Alma cried so much that the guards eventually gave in to her pleas.
Gloria Anzaldúa, a *Chicana* (a woman of Mexican descent, but born
and raised in the United States) writer, once lamented that in her male-
dominated culture, "the [Mexican] Indian woman's only means of
protest was wailing" (1987, p. 21). Alma's wailing prevailed; she and
her husband ended up together again and back in Tiajuana. "That place
is terrible," said Alma. "It's dirty and full of gangs, robbers, and rats."
Yet she felt comforted that at least she and her husband faced its perils
together.

Tiajuana suffers from overpopulation, an overburdened sewage
system, continuous hillside erosion, and wind-blown pollution from

the foul air of Los Angeles. Although there is a sanitized tourist section of the city, the scenic Tiajuana is not the experience of the thousands of illegal aliens who cross the border into the United States monthly. Estimates are that over 3 million illegal immigrants cross the 17-mile strip from the Otay Mountains to the Pacific Ocean, 90% of them on Tiajuana's Mesa de Otay. Another 25 million legal crossings occur each year through a 24-lane system of car entry and another five lanes for pedestrians. It is described as "the busiest stretch of human traffic across a political border anywhere in the world" (Weisman & Dusard, 1986, p. 174). Gangs in Tiajuana prey on frightened and naive undocumented migrants, raping and robbing them. Some of the bandits doing this turn out to be Tiajuana police. The Tiajuana police department, known to have chronic corruption problems, has had a long succession of police chiefs as scandals periodically break out (Weisman & Dusard, 1986).

Alma and Alejandro's third try at the Tiajuana border was finally the one that brought them successfully into California. "This time we didn't have to swim across that river," Alma almost whispered as she remembered.

A street gang in Tiajuana had stopped them and noticed Alma's earrings. "Imagine, I was so naive I didn't even know you should never keep any jewelry on there." A young woman, she thought a *Chicana*, saw what was going on and interceded for them, saying that her earrings were better than Alma's. "Take mine," she told the gang and spared Alma yet another robbery in Tiajuana.

"Maybe she felt sorry for us," said Alma. "But I know she also was attracted to my husband. She asked Alejandro to take her dancing while she thought I was asleep. I think she knew that Alejandro would have fought the gang and gotten hurt badly. But, well, she said she'd help us find a good *coyote* and she did."

"This time," explained Alma, "the *coyote* said he would get us across the border through *la linea* instead of through the countryside." *La linea* was the official border with 2 dozen car lanes stationed by the border patrol. They went in two cars; Alma with the woman who had helped them and Alejandro with the *coyote*. They were instructed to answer the patrolman's query as to where they were going by saying "*con la Joanna*" ["with Joanna"]. The password worked. Bribery, smuggling, gun and drug running are all a part of life at *la frontera*. Although guards on the Mexican side of the border earn only a fraction of what their American counterparts do in salary, they can easily boost their income through monetary bribes and smuggled materials.

Alma and Alejandro spent 2 days at a dropoff house in Los Angeles. This is often part of the *coyote's* service to the migrants. Alma reminisced, "Imagine it, Christina. I was so scared and crazy by the time I got to L.A. that when they let me take a bath, I used the dish detergent to wash with!" She pointed to the bottle of Dawn on the shelf above her own kitchen sink near where I sat writing and laughed out loud. "Sometimes I think they should make a movie out of the story of my honeymoon! I really do," she sighed.

"But, Chris," she looked toward her husband sitting at the other end of the kitchen table, "I want to tell you that before we tried to cross, my husband took me to Morelia." Morelia is the capital of their state and is known for its old world charm and heavily Spanish influence (Foster & Foster, 1993).

"We stayed at a beautiful hotel. We had a beautiful room with a beautiful bathroom. We even had food brought right to the room." They both smiled.

From Los Angeles, Alejandro wired his sister in Chicago to whom he had given some money to save for him. Alejandro had lived in Chicago for 5 years before he returned to Mexico and met and married Alma. She explained that he had won some money on a lottery ticket. He lost part of the money to a female *coyota* in Texas who promised to fill out marriage papers so that he would become legal but instead fled with his $1,500. Not only do illegal aliens fall prey to American mistreatment, but they also suffer at the hands of their own countrymen and -women. So common is the practice that an area outside of Tiajuana, in the "promised land" of the United States, is locally called Smuggler's Canyon. Here refugees are routinely accosted by Mexican robbers who steal, rape, and sell women into prostitution (Anzaldúa, 1987).

Most of the rest of the money Alejandro won and earned he gave to his family back in Juan de Carreo, but he planned ahead and left some with his sister so that she could wire him plane fare to Chicago when he was able to cross again. Alejandro and Alma flew into Chicago and settled in Pilsen, a traditional port of entry for Mexican immigrants, on "*la dieciocho*," as 18th Street is called by the locals. The newlywed couple, within only 3 days of exploitation at the border and 3 hours on an airplane, found themselves freed of the poverty of life on a ranch in the heart of Mexico to face the new experience of urban poverty on Chicago's west side. For Alma, the changes were tremendous. It was there that their first son, Alejandro Jr., was born in 1979.

Two years later, Alma would make the journey back to her hometown, to see her dying father. Upon hearing of her father's illness,

Alejandro told her to go ahead immediately and he would follow with their son the next month. Although Alma complains of having a bad memory, she recalled the exact dates on which they both arrived in Juan de Carreo.

Her father died before she got back. Reunited with Alejandro, she grieved with relatives and within 3 months set out to return to Chicago. They paid a man their families knew $3,000 to bring Alejandro, Jr. back to Alma's brother in Chicago by plane. Alejandro, Jr. was legally a U.S. citizen, but Alma and Alejandro, Sr. still were not and could not bring their own son back to his homeland themselves.

This time Alma and Alejandro crossed at San Diego with about 50 other people in a *coyote's* trailer. They still had to get through a barbed wire fence, and this one was charged with electricity.

"I got lots of shocks where I first tried to get through," she recalled. "But I saw an open spot by some rocks that looked like they'd be easy to slide down quickly. I got through," she confessed, "because I pushed some other people out of the way." She felt that was bad of her to do, but admitted that she did it. She made a decision and she did what she felt she needed to do. "We had to run across an expressway to a *coyote's* truck that was waiting for us." Their fourth crossing was successful on the first try despite the electric shocks, and they were reunited with their son in Chicago shortly afterward. Alma rubbed her hands as she recounted this crossing, remembering the pain of *los toques* [the shocks].

They then moved further west within Chicago, a typical route for the many Mexican families who initially settle near downtown Chicago in the most densely Latino area of the city. The west side offers better housing and more of a neighborhood within a city atmosphere. Alejandro Jr. attended Aims Elementary, a public school, for kindergarten and half of first grade. He was put into the bilingual program, and Alma said they never reported any kind of behavior or academic problems with him during that time. In fact, the kindergarten teacher said he did well.

By December of Alejandro, Jr.'s first-grade year, Alma had had three more children. "Did we have that many children so quickly?" she asked her husband as she told her story. They both laughed.

"I was always sick during those years," she explained. "I thought I had bronchitis. I decided to go back to Mexico with the four children," she said.

"We found out it was allergies later," said Alejandro, Sr. But at that time they felt that Alma needed a warmer climate to recuperate so she returned to Juan de Carreo with all four of her children. Her husband stayed behind in Chicago to continue working to support them all.

It was at a Catholic elementary school in Alma's hometown that she would first hear of her oldest son's problems in reading. The nuns said that they would promote Alejandro to second grade only if he "got help during the summer, you know, like you help him, Chris," explained Alma.

"Did they think it was because he came from the states?" I asked.

"Yes, that's what they said," Alma agreed. The nuns also told her that Alejandro was very well behaved but easily distracted by the other children. "They said he confused some words," she remembered. "And he confused *b*'s and *d*'s," added Alejandro, Sr. "Yes," said Alma, "he confused some numbers, too." Alejandro, Sr. noticed that his son still confuses some letters.

"The nuns said he seemed to like school but he missed his father a lot," Alma recalled.

In December 1986, Alejandro, Sr., who had gotten his "papers" by then and was no longer an illegal alien in U.S. eyes, came to spend the holidays with his family. He wanted them all to return to Chicago but Alma was still sick and wanted to remain in Mexico. Within 2 months, he got a bigger apartment on the west side and Alma sent the children to him. Alejandro continued to coax her to come back because the U.S. government had lifted some restrictions and it was easier to get "papers" during that period—easier to get out from under the stigma of being an illegal *alien*, an ironically dehumanizing term more commonly used to describe space invaders.

"I was sick and I just didn't want to face that river again," she said. "But I remembered what the priest in my hometown had told me: You must follow him and stay with him wherever he goes." Alma seemed to remember his words verbatim. She had told me earlier that day that her oldest sister, who raised her after her mother's tragic death due to erroneous medication given by the town doctor, did not approve of her marriage to Alejandro. She felt that Alejandro was very handsome and probably had another woman, maybe even a wife, from his earlier years in Chicago. In addition, they only dated for 2 months and she refused to let them go ahead with their plans for a church wedding.

So Alma went to their local priest and talked over her problem with him. He agreed to marry them but told Alma that she had to be committed to staying with her husband, she had to follow him wherever he went. She took this advice to heart.

So, alone, Alma had to cross "that river" again. Actually, this crossing was at the Río Grande, for she found a female *coyota* who agreed to get her all the way to Chicago, through Brownsville, Texas, for $1,300.

"This time I came in a train through Brownsville," she laughed as she noted that she used so many types of transportation to cross the border. "I went from the river to a little truck that was waiting for us. We stayed one night in a hotel and then went by train to Chicago. The *coyota* said there were a lot of immigration agents in the airport so that's why we went by train. But I think it was just to save money."

During the time they were separated, her husband had sent her cassettes and pretty, romantic cards, she told me. "I bought some really pretty high heel shoes in Mexico, snake skin high heels. I was crazy. I thought they were just so nice. I packed a little backpack with these fancy shoes and some clothes so I could change after the river, I thought, in the airport. I wanted to look nice for him. Well, the river was so high and I was having trouble breathing and I lost the shoes, the whole backpack. And, you know, the *coyota's* friend charged me $20 for a cheap, pair of plastic sandals she had. But, well, what could I do? I needed shoes."

"They're terrible, those *coyotas*, aren't they?" I asked. "After paying $1,300, they charge you $20 more for sandals?"

"They're bandits," replied Alejandro. "And they live in big beautiful homes in the hills of beautiful towns near the border, on lakes or with pools."

"They prey on their own people," I said. He agreed. But Alma did not. "They're *Chicanos* or *Pochos*" [Americanized Mexicans], she said. She drew this distinction between Mexican born and raised versus Mexican-Americans.

"Well, they have relationships with Americans on the other side, too," said Alejandro. "They're terrible."

This was the last of Alma's border stories. When she got back to Chicago in 1986 she finally filed for and got her "papers." Her fifth child was born an official American citizen. For her, the 2,000-mile border between Mexico and the United States had lived up to its reputation for being an outstanding example of the most dramatic intersection of first and third world realities, "the cutting edge that exposes the nerve endings of two cultures" (Weisman & Dusard, 1986, p. 11).

Her border stories are important to me and important, I believe, to the story of her son, Alejandro. They help me to understand how she and her husband can do factory and restaurant work 10, 12, 16, even 18 hours a day, almost without stop, to ensure financial support for their children. They give me some comprehension of how extremely difficult survival must have been in their homeland for them to have undergone what they did, again and again, at that river, over and under those fences. Anzaldúa calls the U.S.–Mexican border "*una herida abierta* [an open wound] where the Third World grates against the First and bleeds" (1987, p. 3). These experiences also speak to me of family ties so strong that they can withstand the guarantee of physical pain, the possibility of loss of life, as everything is risked to visit a dying parent. And they give me a better understanding, perhaps, of from where their son's resilience emanates, of how a child can throw himself into the face of academic challenges so great that most adolescents would turn to gangs or drugs or truancy. Yet, again and again, like his parents in their persistent journeys through polluted water and electrically charged fences, he tries to succeed academically.

"Look, Chris," Alejandro told me between his mother's stories of the border. "I got C in reading in summer school, and a 2. That's good, isn't it? Look what Mrs. Wright wrote. Right? She says I'm doin' better in reading?"

"This is great, Alejandro," I said. "She finally noticed how much you've improved and how hard you try. A C is much better than an F; you're right." Alejandro had received nothing but F's from this teacher all year. And 2 meant "expected effort" instead of the 3's, meaning "little effort," that Alejandro had received all through eighth grade. The teacher wrote on his report card: "Alejandro's reading ability seems to have improved considerably." This positive comment from his teacher was a major accomplishment for Alejandro. Perhaps his parents have taught him a lesson far greater than help in textual literacy, which they cannot provide. Maybe he has learned from them that if you're strong enough to dive into that river enough times, sooner or later you just might beat the current and succeed in *la lucha* [the struggle].

City of Neighborhoods

We will watch strangers arriving, generation after generation, as boundaries of old communities are breached.
                                    —*The Dialectic of Freedom*, M. Greene

January 12, 1993
    wen I was goin to cach the bus I was waring wead my frend but then
subeli the police stops and they aske questions about if herd guns but
weside No. But stared to se if we haed anithing wead us but weaderent
they leaft and I weant home.
    [When I was going to catch the bus I was waiting with my friend.
But then suddenly the police stops and they ask questions about if heard
guns. But we said, no. But started to see if we had anything with us. But
we didn't. They left and I went home.]
                                    —Alejandro Juarez, Jr., journal entry

Growing up Latino in Chicago, the "City of Neighborhoods" (Pacyga
& Skerrett, 1986), is hard. One out of every three children lives in
poverty (Kotlowitz, 1992; Robles, 1988); approximately 20% of
Chicago's Mexican families and 32% of Puerto Rican families are classified as poor (Robles, 1988). But, in many ways, poverty is not the
greatest problem Latinos face in Chicago.
    The journal entry above was written by the 13-year-old son of Alma
and Alejandro Juarez, who so persistently followed a dream *al norte*
[to the north] with hopes of economic security and an education for
their children. Despite 7 years of schooling in this country, Alejandro
still struggled greatly with English literacy. Experts in ESL predict 5 years
for the kind of language proficiency needed to succeed academically in
a second language (Wong-Fillmore, 1986), yet for Alejandro this was
an underestimate.
    The incident he tries to relate in his journal entry is a frightening
one, yet typical in many ways if you are a male Latino adolescent living
in Chicago. It was Alejandro's mother who told me what happened

before I read of it in his journal. Alejandro and his friend, while waiting for a public bus on the corner near their school, were stopped and frisked by two police officers. Two Latino youths were reported to have fired a gun in the area so Alejandro and his friend, simply by their Latino-ness, became suspects.

"I'm so scared, Christina," Alma told me on the phone. "I don't think they have the right to just do that to my son."

"That's so frightening," I responded. "I don't think they legally can do something like that either; Alejandro must have been terrified."

"Now I'm so worried about sending him home from school on the bus but we have to," lamented his mother. His dad was working overtime and could no longer pick him up after school. "My husband and I are so afraid for him."

The move earlier that school year from an apartment near downtown Chicago to a house in the Brighton Park neighborhood was made with high expectations by Alma and her husband. Both areas have experienced a surge in Latino population in the past 10 years. South Lawndale, the census district that encompasses many of the west side Mexican neighborhoods, has seen a 24% increase in its Latino population from 1980 to 1990; Brighton Park's Latino population rose 167% during the same time period (U.S. Census Bureau, 1991). It appeared to be a popular emigration route within a city well accustomed to waves of ethnic changes in and out of neighborhoods.

Southwest of the center of Chicago, Brighton Park has become a "suburb" of South Lawndale, Pilsen, and the Back of the Yards area. Alma and Alejandro's family and Alma's sister now share a house, which they pooled their money to purchase.

At the beginning of the twentieth century, Brighton Park saw a boom in affordable two-flat housing, which attracted working-class families from the Chicago stockyards. Poles formed the largest ethnic group in the 1930s (Pacyga & Skerrett, 1986). Now, at the end of the twentieth century, the area is experiencing a surge in two new ethnic groups, Latinos (167%) and Asians (69%), who are attracted by the same pleasant housing and easy access to downtown Chicago. Meanwhile, the white population has declined by 24% (U.S. Census Bureau, 1991).

Archer Avenue, a diagonal thoroughfare, cuts a southwestern path extending from State and 19th Street, running beside Chinatown, through Pilsen, Bridgeport, and the Back of the Yards neighborhoods to Brighton Park, eventually ending at the suburb of Summit. Shops and restaurants on Archer in Brighton Park display an array of ethnic backgrounds. Joining Polish-owned businesses and signs advertising *Zimne Piwo* [Cold Beer] on local taverns and *Mowimy Po Polsku* [Pol-

ish spoken] on chains such as Walgreens, are *taquerías* [small taco res-
taurants], Chinese restaurants, and storefront signs decreeing *Se habla
español* [Spanish spoken]. Although the cost of the move and new home
in Brighton Park for the Juarez family would necessitate switching their
four younger children from private to public school, Alma had been
assured by her sister that the public school in the area was a good one.

The bus became a necessity for Alejandro's trip to Sorrowful
Mother when Alejandro's father took on a second job around the
Christmas holidays and could no longer pick him up in the old neigh-
borhood after work.

"Alejandro, promise me that you won't wear your new Bulls jacket
when you have to take the bus," I found myself saying. "I'm just afraid
something might happen to you; somebody might try to hurt you to
get that jacket." The jacket was a prized possession, a Christmas gift
from his parents, who now literally worked day and night to support
their family. The bus Alejandro usually rode took a route across California Avenue in front of the Cook County jail and courthouse complex, an ominous set of buildings with pockets of brick walls topped
with spirals of barbed wire. Traffic always seemed congested in front
of that long block; construction dotted the area. There were days when
I gave Alejandro a ride home when it would take 20 minutes just to
travel that one bustling, barbed wire block. I feared for what could
happen to a boy traveling alone there, sporting a brand-new Chicago
Bulls jacket.

I tried to imagine how I would feel knowing that my children could
be mistaken for gun-bearing juvenile delinquents on the corner near
their own school. In my world as a child and now as a parent, a school
corner was a protected place, a safe haven for students at the end of
the school day. The worst danger it harbored was the ebb and flow of
peer pressure or ridicule. But my "block" was never in Chicago, my
children's skin is white, their hair of blonde and light brown hues, their
language mainstream English. Alejandro's shiny black hair, tanned skin,
and thick Spanish accent easily marked him as nonmainstream in a city
not known for its fondness of cultural pluralism.

"I was scared, Chris," Alejandro told me. "I was real scared when
the cops stop us." His large eyes widened. It was one of the many times
I would think of the deer-like quality of those eyes, the innocence and
vulnerability I saw in them. Alejandro is not expressive with language,
particularly written English language, which is laboriously difficult for
him. But he is very expressive facially, nonverbally. And there are many
times when his silence speaks louder than words. I was struck by how
little he actually spoke of his frightening experience being frisked at

the bus stop, by how little he wrote in his journal entry reflecting that event.

Has he stoically accepted his status in the community where he is pegged as a probable juvenile delinquent just by virtue of his Latino features? Like his parents, has he learned to enfold the difficult and disappointing into his life without letting it overpower him, as a cook folds fragile ingredients gently into the larger batter.

His simple rendition of his school corner ordeal, one winter afternoon on his way home, belies the fear I saw in his eyes and heard in his mother's voice. Routinely, I fear, he masks the problems he faces on the streets, assimilates them into the lived experience that is his. Being Latino in Chicago neighborhoods is not easy.

Sorrowful Mother and Sister

The students stirred restlessly. . . . I took a quick look around me. It reminded me of a chocolate sundae. All the pale-faced Anglos were the
vanilla ice cream, while we brown-faced Hispanos were the sauce. The
nun, with her starched white headdress under her cowl, could have been
the whipped cream except that I figured she was too sour for that. . . .
Sister Mary Margaret welcomed us to class. "You are here," she said, "as
good Catholic children to learn your lessons well so you can better wor-
ship and glorify God." Ominous words in Anglo that I understood too
well. I knew that cleanliness was next to godliness. But I never knew that
learning your school lessons was—until then.
      —*The Day the Cisco Kid Shot John Wayne*, N. Candelaria

Sorrowful Mother School is one of many west side Chicago Catholic
elementary schools that serve, almost exclusively, low income Latino
children. Their populations are typically 98–99% Latino, 1–2% African-
American, with an occasional newly emigrated Eastern European student. Many of the parishes to which these schools are connected were
Eastern European at the turn of the century, when they were built.
Names of Slavic parishes—Adalbert, Ludmilla, Cyril, Procopius—
remain anomalous reminders of earlier immigrant groups. Since the
period surrounding the Haymarket Riot of 1886 in Pilsen, when Eastern
European labor leaders accused of being anarchists clashed with police
and conservative business owners, there has been a long and strong
history of Slavic (particularly Bohemian and Polish) influence in the
now predominantly Latino lower west side, which radiates south toward
the South Lawndale, Bridgeport, and Brighton Park neighborhoods.
Although the white population has decreased in the past 10 years in
Pilsen by 49%, in South Lawndale by 60%, and in the Brighton Park
area by 24%, a recent wave of Polish immigrants promises to revive an
earlier tradition, particularly in the area surrounding Crown High
School on a main thoroughfare near these areas (U.S. Census Bureau,
1991).

26

The Catholic Archdiocese of Chicago educates approximately 21,000 Latino elementary school children in these and other ethnic neighborhoods, and feels a strong commitment to what it calls its Hispanic ministry (Data and Research Office, Archdiocese of Chicago, personal communication). In fact, some recent statistics attest to the effectiveness of Catholic education for Latinos. Valerie Lee, using test scores provided by the National Assessment of Educational Progress, found that Latino Catholic school students scored significantly above the national average for all Latino students at the seventh-, eighth-, and eleventh-grade levels (Valdivieso, 1986). Lee herself points out the problem of selectivity bias in these statistics as the range of Latino students is narrower in Catholic schools. Yet when researcher William R. Morgan (1983) statistically accounted for these factors, Catholic education still emerged stronger in verbal achievement gains for Latino students who came from homes where Spanish is the principal language spoken, which is often the lowest scoring group nationally.

Historically, Mexicans have felt strong ties to Catholicism and parochial education, a legacy left them by their Spanish conquistadors. They have made Catholicism uniquely their own, particularly in their devotion to Our Lady of Guadalupe. She is their version of the Blessed Mother imbued with Indian elements, emblematic of the country's fervent devotion and faith in God despite the hardships and poverty they routinely face.

Mexican parents will take extra jobs, fund raise, and work in these schools as cafeteria and clerical aides, even as custodial help, to ensure a Catholic education for their children. Theirs is an active religion, one woven visibly into the fabric of their lives. *"Si Dios quiere"* ["if God wills"] and *"Dios nos va a ayudar"* ["God will help us"] are everyday expressions in conversation. Every Mexican home I have visited as a teacher in Chicago always proudly displays *La Virgen de Guadalupe*, in pictures or statues, often in the living room. *Taquerías* and record shops, *carnicerías* [butchers] and *panaderías* [bakeries] frequently include an image of the beloved Mexican mother intermingled with their products. A small *taco parado* [quick serve taco shop] on Blue Island Avenue, a major thoroughfare linking Pilsen to downtown Chicago, juxtaposes a portrait of a bull fighter, a mounted bull's head, and the Virgin of Guadalupe above the jukebox. She has been called the most national symbol that exists for a beleaguered country (Rodriguez, 1992).

After Alma's younger children switched to the public school system earlier in the year, she told me that she doesn't bother to hang their work on her refrigerator anymore. "When they went to Catholic school, they would bring home nice pictures of Our Lady of Guadalupe, with flowers, they were very nice. I'd hang them up. But now, they bring pictures of men with big *machetes* [knives]. I don't want to hang those things up," lamented Alma.

Sorrowful Mother does a good job of passing on "that old-fashioned religion" to its students. This is an area of good cultural congruity for Sorrowful Mother students between their community and school lives. Pictures of Mexico's Virgin abound as do other religious statues and pictures left over from Slavic immigrants years ago. Colorful *sombreros* [straw hats] and *zarapes* [cloaks] adorn the halls and give public acknowledgment of the Mexican culture. The children attend Mass and Reconciliation, learn church songs, and have *fiestas* [parties] surrounding religious holiday themes. These are activities that are prized by the Mexican families that support them. A Mexican mother from a different Catholic school once complained to me that some of her son's teachers didn't even start the class day with prayers and that they wanted to do away with confessions during school hours. Going to confession is indeed a fading practice in the modern Catholic church.

"We Mexican parents don't want to do away with those things; they're important to us," she said. "I spoke up about that and told them at a meeting." Even a very quiet woman, very traditionally respectful to clergy, found her voice in terms of her conception of faith.

At Sorrowful Mother, Sister Mary Eleanor, the principal, was the heart and soul of the religious education curriculum. She was the core, defender, and enforcer of religion throughout the building. Of Slavic background herself, she was trilingual and spoke English, Czech, and Spanish. To her credit, she was one of many Catholic administrators in the area who have learned their new immigrant students' language.

Unlike other principal nuns I have observed, who have embraced an updated, warmer, less didactic version of Catholicism, Eleanor had a clear and traditional vision of her religion and imposed it, without batting an eye, upon her charges. The key word for me here is *imposes*. Hers is not a particularly gentle faith—at times I heard her berate a student for poor academic work, calling upon him to straighten out for his parents' sake, his own, and God's. God seemed to get called into play a lot in her scoldings. And few escaped her scoldings. Students, parents, teachers, and aides, at one time or another, are the recipients of her booming orders that echo through the tall old hallways of Sorrowful Mother. Yet there have been times when I heard Sister Eleanor teaching young students lovely, community-centered religious songs in their own language, or just recounting stories of her faith sweetly and lovingly. At these moments I have felt that there is no one

else in the whole city who could do a better job of expressing to children sheer love and faith in a warm, embracing God. To me, she is a
walking contradiction. For I have heard her, angry with children or
their parents, chastise and lecture vehemently and condescendingly,
calling into play her position as a religious, which often paralyzes
Mexican children and their parents into submission taught them historically by the Catholic Church. Waiting to speak to Eleanor outside
her office one day, I heard her lecture a robust junior high student and
both his parents regarding the changes she deemed necessary in his life
in order to improve his school performance. All three members of this
Mexican family sat, heads bowed, repentantly looking at the floor as
she decreed that no television should be allowed during the weekdays
and that the son absolutely had to shape up and do better in school.
At times I convinced myself that her bark is worse than her bite, but at
other moments I could not condone the repercussions of her strong
opinions and the punishments she doles out. I have seen the consequences experienced by Alejandro in particular as she vacillates between
viewing him as a student with special academic needs and one who just
does not try hard enough.

There is a curious tone to the school. On the one hand, the Mexican artifacts and accessibility to the Spanish language bespeak acceptance and a sense of community but on the other hand there is a clear
sense of "them" and "us." "Those" who need to be educated and "we"
who possess the knowledge, the brains, the right way of doing things.
Although there are staff and volunteers who speak Spanish, Eleanor
strongly espoused an immersion approach to learning English. She
proudly boasted that students at Sorrowful Mother learn English because they are immersed in it, while those at the nearby public school,
which has a bilingual program, do not. And she is correct. Mexican
parents, in frustration, have switched their children from the public
school to the private school after noticing firsthand that they are not
learning English. This is a common complaint of parents on the west
side, including Alejandro's parents, who are concerned that their children learn English so as to advance economically in the future. The
need for English in order to succeed in the workplace is a reality with
which they personally deal daily. Bilingual programs in Chicago often
pay little attention to English as a Second Language needs, relegating
English to one 40-minute ESL period a day or less that is not integrated
with their regular curriculum. A shortage of competent ESL teachers is
a common plight, and bilingual education in Chicago public schools
is frequently, in effect, monolingual Spanish language education
through fourth grade. Although a firm basis in the first language is very

helpful when transitioning to the second language, parents become anxious when they perceive a lack of a systematic entry into English.

All content areas in Sorrowful Mother, however, are taught in English; Eleanor saw to that, even for students newly entering directly from Mexico. Only in kindergarten will bilingual teachers who use Spanish be found, and some teachers on the staff disagree with that situation, feeling that it just delays English usage unnecessarily. The Spanish that is allowed seems to be connected to cultural and religious events and ceremonies, and Eleanor was as strong in seeing that it *is* included as she is in demanding English immersion in the content areas.

Sister Eleanor did, however, fight to get an English as a Second Language program in her school through a local university when she heard about such a program offered in a nearby Catholic school. She persistently called the dean of education, reminding him of the university's Catholic, urban mission and her own order's affiliation with it in a graduate program. The dean finally gave permission to extend the small field-based ESL program to Eleanor's school, stating frankly that he was weary of the badgering by phone. Yet, once the ESL program arrived, Eleanor gradually made her disapproval of it apparent. The program was anchored in a whole language approach to second language learning. Strongly convinced that a skills and remedial approach is needed for second language literacy, she supported the program only half-heartedly. Her view of language was not developmental; instead, she saw the English language as a set of skills to be drilled and mastered. She complained that the students missed too much of their regular classes when ESL was offered for three 40-minute sessions a week and preferred a once-a-week meeting schedule. As director of that program I voiced my concern over the efficacy of a once weekly curriculum, and a twice weekly compromise was reached. Regular classroom teachers were asked to collaborate with ESL teachers so as to link ESL themes with their main curriculum, but little input was provided by Sorrowful Mother's faculty. Children frequently were missing from ESL classes whenever regular classroom activities made them inconvenient. Even students with the most minimal English comprehension and expression were kept from ESL classes. This, indeed, was the experience of Alejandro, who frequently needed the ESL teacher to request permission for him to attend the ESL class, which often was denied.

Sister Eleanor and her staff complained that the ESL program did not produce visible results, and the ESL teachers assigned to Sorrowful Mother pointed out that the refusal of regular teachers to consistently send children even twice weekly greatly hindered the positive effect the program could feasibly have on them. Absenteeism by frustrated graduate students working in the ESL program further hindered progress. It was a sad situation for the many children, including Alejandro, who needed ESL help and were adversely affected by the lack of agreement on how to construct that help.

Sister Eleanor followed the same pattern regarding remedial reading classes. Although the Archdiocese has clear guidelines on the amount of help to be received by children diagnosed with reading needs, Eleanor hired a remedial reading teacher to meet with students once a week for 50 minutes. Despite the remedial reading teacher's attempts to convince her that a once-a-week program was ineffective, Eleanor refused to extend the time. Although the reading teacher struggled to offer a whole language literacy program, using relevant children's literature, teachers told her that Sister Eleanor insisted on a skills approach in their classrooms. Any hint of whole language was considered an extra, if time permitted.

Eleanor once told me that her students get remedial reading and computer training once a week. She felt that along with a once weekly ESL session, the combination of "specials" should take care of any problems. If it didn't, in her opinion, it was usually because the student didn't try hard enough. Eleanor had reasoning behind what she did; there always was a philosophy underlying her actions. Pullout programs do pose problems to homeroom teachers who lose students for blocks of time, yet there was even more resistance from the Sorrowful Mother staff to inclusive models in which special educators, like ESL teachers, can integrate their classes with regular education. Although the staff acknowledged their need for certain expertise, there also existed a feeling of not wanting anybody to interfere with the Sorrowful Mother way of educating.

The majority of regular educators at Sorrowful Mother, particularly in middle and junior high grades, ran a tight ship. For more than 4 years I had observed them discipline students rigorously in the corridors and detention halls. From the ESL classroom I could hear neighboring teachers shout at and berate children. Teachers enforced silence, speed, individual accomplishments, punctuality in assignment completion, and obedience. Punishment for infractions was public—verbal corrections and after-school detentions were given; as a punishment older students sometimes were sent to the kindergarten rooms to complete work and be publicly humiliated by sitting with the younger children.

Some attempts at collaborative grouping were made in the school, although the grouping I witnessed at the junior high level typically involved only physically creating the group. Once students were arranged as groups, the teacher then did separate work, often using the time to correct papers or tidy an area of the classroom. I observed Mrs. Wright, Alejandro's main teacher, conduct such grouping in a social studies class. She kept busy during the groupwork with paperwork of her own and monitoring the students' behavior. But her interaction with the groups regarding the project at hand was limited; she appeared to expect the students to know how best to divide assignments and complete the tasks. Yet, it seemed clear to me as an observer that most of the groups were not working efficiently or collaboratively. Usually one student wrote and the others sat and watched. They argued a bit about what should be copied, then sat and waited for one member to do it, although there were other coloring, printing, and cutting tasks that needed to be done. The teacher oversaw the groups rather than helping them to organize further or create activities particularly amenable to cooperative work, a situation not uncommon in classrooms where cooperative grouping is a new concept.

Sister Eleanor's educational convictions greatly affected Alejandro, who fell into her category of a student who just did not try hard enough despite the three weekly "specials" he received. In reality, Alejandro was rarely present in ESL class and only periodically present in remedial reading. Regular class activities interfered with his specials times. The last thing Alejandro needed was to fall even further behind in his regular classes, yet even custodial assignments he had in the afternoons superseded reading or ESL needs. Computer training, which was a whole-class period, was the only special he consistently attended during school hours. Games and worksheet-formatted extensions of his classwork were offered there; the strong skills base of the school was apparent in the choice of computer materials.

After-school tutoring was the only consistent specialized help Alejandro received and even that was constrained by the days Sister Eleanor would allow me to stay and work with him. During fall and winter, Wednesday, when another teacher held a special remedial class to prepare low achieving eighth graders for the Catholic High School Entrance Exam, was the day I had permission to work with Alejandro from 2:45 until 4:00. We had to persistently remind that teacher, who locked the building and set its alarms at the end of the day, that we were working in the ESL room. Even with these reminders, she left early one fall afternoon, locking us in the building. Unaware, we proceeded to walk downstairs at 4:00 to the main exit and tripped the light-sensitive alarm at the bottom of the stairway. A deafening siren went off, scaring both of us as we tripped several more and with our hands covering our ears ran out the back exit. Like a repentant puppy I ran to the nearby convent and begged the reluctant cook to call Sister Eleanor for me so that she could turn off the alarm system. Mr. Juarez was there to pick up Alejandro and he too explained the urgency of our problem to the cook.

"Sister Eleanor isn't answering her call," she told us. The nuns have a system of bell signals to which they respond, but Eleanor, who was in the building, did not answer her coded call.

After pleading unsuccessfully with the cook to disturb Sister Eleanor and explaining that the alarm was still ringing, I finally said, "Well, I'm not waiting any longer; we did all that we could."

"*La otra maestra* [the other teacher] left a little before 4:00," Mr. Juarez told me. "I saw her leave. She must have forgotten you were there." We left as the alarm continued its deafening ring. From that point on, Alejandro and I always left a little earlier than 4:00.

After the entrance exam preparation class ended, things got worse. We now could work together only on Thursdays, when group detentions were held from 2:45–3:45. With an even greater chance of being forgotten and locked in the building by the rotating detention proctors, Alejandro and I worked in a corner of the cafeteria where silent detention took place. This was somewhat distracting to Alejandro but the local library was even more noisy to work in. Toward the end of the year, detention proctors became more lax and we would work alone in the lunchroom, always listening to be sure that someone was still in the building. One day they forgot to tell us that the exterminators were coming, and as we sat and read in the cafeteria corner, workmen in overalls came and began to spray around us. That day we worked in my car.

The message we received was implicit but strong. This tutoring for Alejandro was superfluous, was clearly neither Sister Eleanor's nor his teacher's priority.

Despite his remedial status and the frequent disciplining he received, Alejandro felt at home in Sorrowful Mother. There he was protected from gang violence during school hours, for Sister Eleanor absolutely would not tolerate any hint of gang activity in her building. This is no small accomplishment for a principal in the west side of Chicago.

Alejandro also saw great connections between his parents' religious convictions and those of Sister Eleanor. Faith was important; faith was central to school and home life; faith was tied to culture.

"Sister Eleanor talked to us for a long time after Mass," Alejandro would tell me. Ostensibly, she wove education and religion together in her lectures, which seemed to alternate between sermons and motivational talks with a little dose of the fear of the Lord thrown in. Although he was afraid of his principal, Alejandro also appreciated the perquisites she loved to give her students—donated candy from a local factory, all-school field trips, an eighth-grade party on ribbon day. These were clearly treats from Sister Eleanor, and for Alejandro and many of the other students, the treats seemed to smooth their perceptions of her. They seemed to compensate for her brashness, which, on one occasion during that year, had culminated in the alleged slapping of a student. She was, as I said, a walking contradiction in my eyes.

Although I cannot condone her behavior toward children and parents, or agree with the educational policies she set in motion and dictated at Sorrowful Mother, I am sure of one strangely dichotomous fact. She loved and was totally dedicated to the school and the Mexican community she served—of that I am convinced. Her pride in a clean, well-organized and maintained school was clearly evident; her conviction in her educational and curricular beliefs sincere and strong. And Alejandro, like many other students, will always remember her with a curious mixture of appreciation and apprehension.

Uncommon Ground

I was totally immersed *en lo mexicano* [in the "Mexican"].
—*Tlilli Tlappalli*, G. Anzaldúa

It all began with *The Ugly Duckling*. I was working with Alejandro on a series of paperback books for second language learners during our after-school tutoring sessions in the fall. The series had simplified some of the traditional Western classics (*Little Women, A Christmas Carol, Black Beauty*) for second language readers. They were packaged in adult-looking formats, yet the vocabulary was at a primary level. Although the texts lost much of their linguistic richness and presented only Western European-based literature, I felt that they at least provided second language readers with an introduction to some wonderful stories at a comprehensible reading level without looking babyish. I had chosen a set of Hans Christian Anderson stories, feeling that the length of each selection was good for Alejandro, whose attention span, especially after a full day's schoolwork, was limited. I also envisioned Alejandro reading the short stories to his younger brother and sisters, who had no home story reading experiences due to their parents' textual illiteracy. I was hoping for a trickle down effect from big brother to younger siblings.

Alejandro dutifully read the first story, *The Ugly Duckling*, but his blank expression betrayed his lack of comprehension.

"Have you ever seen a swan?" I asked. I translated the word for him into Spanish. "*Un cisne*," I said.

"I don't know that word," Alejandro replied.

I remembered seeing a large poster of a swan in one of the other classrooms so I took him to see it. Still no recognition. I then realized that we were not dealing with a second language problem here. It was a difference in background experiences. I began to explain how swans look compared with ducks and why it was so important to the story.

"I've seen ducks," he said hopefully. He was trying so hard to live up to my expectations for him having seen a swan.

"Maybe some day you and your brother and sisters could come to the zoo near my house with me and my daughters. They have swans there," I thought out loud. The real thing seemed better than a picture at that moment.

I realized what an unfortunate choice *The Ugly Duckling* story had been. It's hard to appreciate the story with no understanding of swans. It was just one more instance in my teacher–student relationship with Alejandro in which he could interpret himself as failing, although this clearly was my failure. That day, I decided to hold off on any more of the Western Euro-centered classics and try to locate some culturally relevant literature at a comprehensible level. I felt that maybe I had been trying to fit a square peg into a round hole, so to speak.

But I went ahead with the plans for a zoo trip. In late November through December, Brookfield Zoo has an event called "Holiday Magic." For just four weekends, the zoo, which otherwise closes before dark, was open all evening. Thousands of tiny white Christmas lights are strung all over the zoo grounds, ice sculptors demonstrate their craft, Christmas carols play throughout the park, and special activities are set up for children. With a little help from the weather, some snow falls and the place really does look like a winter wonderland. Energetic young zoo guides from the local high schools often lead the visitors in singing carols on the zoo trains and buses. I had fond memories of the special evenings with my children in past years and I wanted to share the event with the Juarez family.

Alma and I finally arrived at a date for my mini-field trip. A teacher friend of mine once told me that her kids' friends used to feel sorry for her children because, they teased, "when your mother's a teacher you never get to just go somewhere for fun, everything's got to be educational." I couldn't resist thinking how great it would be for the Juarez kids to actually experience new vocabulary words, to hear and say *swan* in front of the real McCoy. The ESL teacher in me surfaced but the mom side of me still wanted it all to be fun—even more—holiday fun. I had great expectations.

When I arrived at the Juarez home to pick up Alejandro and his brother and sisters, Alma had just returned from work. Despite just finishing a 10-hour shift, I felt that Alma wanted to join us on our excursion. I was right. Alma jumped at the invitation, quickly brushed her hair, and came along.

Alejandro stuck to her like glue at the zoo. They whispered to each other as we walked from exhibit to exhibit. It was as if they were jointly trying to make sense of this whole, somewhat overwhelming event. Alicia, Ricardo, Almita, and Lupita were literally wide-eyed, taking in all that was going on around them. Following my youngest daughter's cues, Alejandro's youngest sisters and brother excitedly found good vantage points to see the animals, climbing on rocks and boosting on to the lower rungs of fences. Alicia, Alejandro, and Alma kept a watchful eye on the younger kids and responded in a more restrained way to most of the exhibits, but always with wide-eyed interest. In the new "Desert Section," though, Alejandro and Alma openly showed their amazement and enjoyment of the desert creatures, particularly the bats. They laughed and pointed to the creatures, chattering excitedly while watching the large, crow-sized bats that were hanging from a man-made tree. When I expressed my utter dislike of bats, Alejandro enjoyed them even more and teased me for flinching at them as they flew by. I've realized that Alejandro likes to tease. For him, it's a way of showing affection, much as it is for Alma, who lovingly teases her children. One of Alejandro's favorite games at tutoring was to tell me that he had lost his journal. Once he did misplace it temporarily, so his fabricated losses were quite convincing. He delighted in this teasing, always affectionately reassuring me in the end that he would never actually lose the journal after the one genuine scare that took place.

We ended the evening at the Discovery Center where art projects were set up for the youngest children. Alicia, Ricardo, Almita, Lupita, and my younger daughter, Mary, loved the activities and got to use stamps of arctic animals to decorate cards. Alma hesitatingly but knowingly encouraged her children to take advantage of the supplies set out for the projects. Alejandro feigned disinterest but I felt would have loved to dabble in the stamping himself. Instead he discovered a display where pennies would rotate and descend in spiraling circles down a funnel-shaped receptacle. He excitedly fed it with change as Alma looked on with enjoyment equal to his.

As we went from exhibit to exhibit that evening, Alma enjoyed them with her children. I, on the other hand, felt a compulsion to instruct and explain; to read the animal names and descriptions at the various sites. Although this skill is not in Alma's repertoire, she fully participates with her family, enjoying their reactions and reacting quizzically herself as together they experience new things. This spontaneity is something lost in the more traditional, instructive parenting style I see so frequently in my suburban world. Parent is the knower; child is the learner. Parent, like teacher, asks pseudoquestions, as a way to quiz children's learning. Alma, on the other hand, asked her children genuine questions that are real for her, that she sincerely wondered about, as opposed to probes for putative understanding. She and her children discovered new learning together. Sometimes learning opportunities were lost because of the burden of Alma's textual illiteracy. But sometimes, I think, there is a closeness and authenticity in the joy of collaborative discovery that is easily missed by many print literate parents who have had more formal schooling.

All kids love spaghetti—so I thought. After the zoo trip, Alma suggested going to a McDonald's, but I explained that I already had dinner ready and waiting at my home, 5 minutes away. I had changed my mind about ordering pizza for everyone and thought that a home-cooked meal would be more special. I made spaghetti and was careful to put the sauce on the side in case some of the kids (like my own) preferred plain pasta.

We arrived at my home and Alma and her children sat timidly in our family room. Suddenly the three youngest Juarezes gasped and literally ran into a corner behind the couch.

"What's wrong?" I asked in Spanish, and Alejandro pointed to our pet cat who had just strolled into the room.

Alma was embarrassed and tried to get the kids to stop crying and cringing. I immediately put B.C., our loving 17-year-old cat, in the basement, promising the Juarezes that he would never hurt anyone. Alma explained that Alicia had been bitten by a dog on the street once and that since then the younger children were afraid of dogs and cats.

Alicia, Lupita, Almita, and Ricardo sat huddled around Alma once I put B.C. away. It took several minutes of coaxing to get them to believe that our cat was locked away and couldn't get out. My older daughter, Elizabeth, even showed them the closed basement door.

That crisis over, we all sat down for dinner in our dining room. I felt uncomfortable when Alma gazed across our dining room and living room, commenting with genuine awe on how big our house was. I realized that this was the first time she had ever been in a mainstream American suburban home. Compared with the two-flat houses she was accustomed to seeing in South Lawndale for years, few of which had family or dining rooms, my house must have seemed huge. I was embarrassed, for I was acutely aware that, despite the abundance of material possessions she was noticing, I knew of no suburban homes that could compete with the richness of family concern and closeness that existed in hers.

Dinner was a disaster. Contrary to my belief that spaghetti was a universally known, "safe" food to serve children, the Juarez kids looked as if I had served them a plate full of worms. Alma told me that it was her first time having American spaghetti, although she had heard of it.

I served her the pasta and the sauce, and she pleaded quietly with her children to try it.

"It's like ketchup," I heard her whisper to Ricardo, "just put a little of it on."

Alejandro politely took a small portion, then sat and looked at it. Lupita was the only one of the Juarez kids who ate it.

"I thought for sure you would have had spaghetti in your school lunches," I said to Alejandro. I knew they were enrolled in the free lunch program for years at Sorrowful Mother, and spaghetti was always a part of the monthly menus.

"We did, but we just didn't eat it," explained Alejandro. "Only Lupita, she's the only one who eats it."

All the while, Alma kept telling me how much she liked my food and kept coaxing her family to eat it and apologizing to me for their reactions.

Thank goodness for Italian bread. Alicia, Ricardo, Almita, and Alejandro ate that part of the meal. Alicia valiantly tried to convince me that she frequently filled up on bread at meals. Alma agreed. At one point I watched little Ricardo awkwardly try to balance some meatballs on the bread and try to eat them before they rolled off. It reminded me of an experience I had years ago in high school while visiting a friend's family in Puerto Rico. Her parents served fish for dinner; whole fish with the heads still on, which is typical in the Caribbean and Central and South America. I, however, had never seen anything other than tunafish salad or a fish filet. I sort of poked around at my serving, grateful for the side dish of rice, but couldn't face the fish head. My girlfriend's family noticed and coaxed me to try it. Her brother proceeded to demonstrate how the fish eyes were rubbery. He and his pals chewed them like chewing gum. He bounced one on the kitchen floor to show me just how resilient they were. His demonstration didn't help the situation at all!

I saw that same disdain I remembered from my fish head dinner 20 years earlier on the faces of Alejandro and his siblings that night I served them spaghetti. Fish heads to them. At least dessert was well-received; I fed them all the cupcakes I had, hoping that they wouldn't leave my home feeling hungry.

My family and I cleared off the table, and Alma quickly directed her children to help. We all ended up in the kitchen at the dishwasher. My husband and I loaded it up as the entire Juarez family, I realized, crowded around it in amazement. Ricardo could not contain his curiosity.

"Wow," he sighed.

Alicia said proudly, "My father says he work with these at

McCormick Place." Mr. Juarez had found a second job for the holidays at the main restaurant in McCormick Place (a conference center) as a dishwasher. Alma agreed with Alicia, "Yes, he's told us about these."

My husband showed Ricardo, who was tremendously interested in this modern-day marvel, how the dishwasher worked. He stopped it in mid-cycle so that Ricardo could see how the spraying water reached to both levels. Alejandro, his mom, and the girls watched with as much wonder as Ricardo did. Again, I felt uncomfortable. I had a university professor who once told me that I had to think about being white and getting involved with a Latino family. I should really ponder the ramifications of cross-cultural involvement, she felt. She questioned whether I had the right to expose minority children to a more affluent way of life that she felt was out of their reach. I react strongly to this sort of issue for I believe firmly that multicultural education should encourage and facilitate cross-cultural contact and understanding, and sharing. I also think of myself as one human being involved with another and truly look at differences in terms of a richness in diversity, not with judgmental comparisons.

"Boy, would Dr. Jones have had a field day with that scenario around the dishwasher," I said to my husband after the evening was over. "Did I have the right to let them see a way of life they could almost assuredly never have monetarily?" she would have challenged. This was one such issue she had mentioned. I wondered about it all night long. I never wanted the Juarez family to be in awe of anything I had materially, especially not my dishwasher. I do not come from a background of affluence and do not want people to perceive me now as affluent. I see myself as the daughter of blue-collar, working-class parents for whom the gift of education has afforded some small modicum of monetary success. But concerns for affluence and striving for materialistic success are not goals of mine or something with which I want to be associated.

"My house can't compare at all with yours in upkeep," I mentioned to Alma as I drove her home. Despite dishwashers and more space, our housekeeping efforts are meager in comparison to the Juarez house, which is immaculately clean and orderly. This is a point of great pride for Alma. Alejandro and his father do most of the cleaning, not typical in other Mexican households I have visited, but very true in theirs.

"Alejandro will even clean the oven and stove for me while I'm at work," Alma boasted. "He and my husband mop the floors almost every day. They take care of all the housework for me." Alejandro added, "Well, I do it after I do my homework. I have nothing else to do, really. I don't mind." Alma teased and told me that the only thing Alejandro won't do is wash the dishes. "He says that's women's work." We both laughed. Some traditions die harder than others.

So the big zoo excursion was over. Our trip took us on more uncommon ground than I had expected. I believe that I learned more than anyone else on this mini-field trip, a good part of my learning experience occurring in my own kitchen. As I visited the Juarez home more frequently in the months to come and talked more with Alma, I realized just how much "cultural incongruence" I served them at that unsuccessful dinner. Other than pizza, some sweets, and McDonald's hamburgers, the Juarez children truly did not stray far from a Mexican diet. Alma left food cooked for them, when she worked from 3 p.m. to 1 a.m. every day. *Sopa de arroz* [rice with sauce], *frijoles* [beans], *huevos* [eggs], *chayotes* [sweet cactus] and Home Run Inn Pizza with *jalapeños* [chili peppers] added were her children's favorites. Not spaghetti.

Mrs. Wright's Way

The deserving ones, who are they? They are those who obey.
—*Miss Margarida's Way*, R. Athayde

Alejandro did not care for Mrs. Wright's way of teaching. Usually very reluctant to say anything negative about teachers or adults in authority, in the case of his eighth-grade homeroom teacher, Alejandro overcame his reluctance. He searched for affirmation of his negative perceptions of Mrs. Wright. Not critical of treatment in his schooling that many would find degrading, Alejandro seemed to realize that this teacher, at times, crossed the line into inappropriate teacher behavior.

"Right, a teacher shouldn't shove kids? Right, she shouldn't make fun of the way you talk?" Alejandro periodically recounted incidences when his teacher lost her temper and shouted at students, pushed them, and ridiculed their Spanish accents.

"She made a kid cry today, Chris. A boy!" Alejandro confided in me at our tutoring session. "I don't think it's right to make fun of somebody 'cause he doesn't know English. That's what she does sometimes."

"You mean she makes fun of the kids' English in front of the class?" I asked in disbelief.

"Oh yeah, yeah, she does that, Chris, to some of the kids who don't know much English. Right, that's not good for a teacher to do?"

Alejandro frequently phrased his observations and perceptions of these events as questions. Alejandro found a way to avoid troublesome interrogative constructions, which typically present substantial difficulty to second language speakers, by simply prefacing a statement with "Right" and delivering it in a questioning intonation. It got the job done.

Mrs. Wright, a young woman always dressed in perfectly pressed and coordinated clothing, spoke with a pronounced Australian accent. She was formal and businesslike. A covert battle seemed to be waged between her and her students. Her classes were held in absolute silence; perfect obedience was expected from her students. Yet passive-aggressive pranks and behavior would pop up periodically. Chalk wedged in erasers, spit balls tossed, little bits of rebellion that Mrs. Wright indefatigably combated. I spoke to her one afternoon about a punishment assigned to Alejandro, which I found incredibly insensitive to his documented English spelling problems, as she sat at a table with an after-school group of eighth graders she tutored in math. Yes, I had it right, I was assured. Alejandro had to write the names of 40 African and Asian nations and capitals 10 times each "because he had done poorly on a geography quiz." In the evaluation made available to Alejandro's school it was particularly noted that he had tested weakly in the areas of both auditory and visual memory. This problem did not concern Mrs. Wright, not to mention the difficulty in written language from which Alejandro suffered. I asked Mrs. Wright to check the difficult spellings on the list of capitals Alejandro had copied; I wasn't sure of many of them myself and I had hoped she'd change her mind about the punishment knowing that I was aware of it. But she didn't reconsider. As Mrs. Wright hurriedly checked the list, the boys in her tutoring group kicked a box full of books that was under the table into her leg. Thinking I hadn't noticed, Mrs. Wright glared sideways toward them, head still facing the list of countries, and forcefully kicked it right back into their feet as she continued checking Alejandro's spelling. This physical aggression seemed not to faze her one bit. She fought fire with fire.

Long before I entered Mrs. Wright's classroom I had abiding concerns about the kind of teaching she practiced. Although I had planned to work on reading and writing during our tutoring sessions, Alejandro often had homework assignments from Mrs. Wright that were overwhelming, given his trouble with written English.

Alejandro's assignments reflected Mrs. Wright's conception of education. Frequently we spent half of our tutoring time on homework, an almost futile task, and far beyond Alejandro's comprehension most of the time. Early in the fall, Alejandro asked me to help him with a composition he had to do for Mrs. Wright entitled, "A Visit to the Dentist's Office." I quickly realized as we tried to talk about how he felt at the dentist and what he remembered of the office, that Alejandro had never been to a dentist.

"Alejandro, how can you write about something you've never experienced?" I asked.

"We can just make it up, Chris. That's what the kids are doing," he replied.

"Well, have you been to a doctor's office, Alejandro?" I asked.

"Yeah, Chris, I been to the doctor's when I had a bad sore throat," answered Alejandro.

"Why don't you write about that?" I suggested. "If Mrs. Wright gets upset about that, I'll speak with her."

The assignment, taken from an English textbook, had written dialogue as its focus. I didn't think it would matter under which context the dialogue took place. At least Alejandro could pull something of personal meaning into this task.

Most of the homework I would help Alejandro with in the months ahead reflected this kind of absence of connection to anything relevant or meaningful to Alejandro's or his classmates' lives. An outstandingly problematic assignment required the students to critique a newspaper editorial. Again, it was taken directly from their English textbook. Knowing that Alejandro's family did not buy English newspapers, which was not uncommon for Latino families in Chicago, I decided to take him to a store near his school to get one so that he could do his homework. We went to three small grocery stores in the neighborhood and stopped at several newspaper machines along the main thoroughfare and could not find a single English newspaper for the assignment. We had to drive out of the barrio into a nearby African-American neighborhood before we found an English newspaper at a gas station mart. I wondered what the other students in Alejandro's class would do since they all lived near the school and did not easily cross neighborhood and gang lines. And Mrs. Wright did not use anything of the Spanish language for instruction. The editorials we did find were so far beyond Alejandro's English proficiency, the vocabulary so demanding, it seemed a futile exercise once again. "I'll bring in the page," said Alejandro. At least it was proof of his effort to accomplish the latest task. He always found ways to cope academically, even if just marginally.

Another particularly difficult assignment required that Alejandro write a summary of a Greek myth told orally by his Australian teacher to his class of totally Mexican students; no notes were allowed to be taken. The students were following a system of memorization called TRACK, which relied completely on auditory memory as if there were only one true way to remember lectures.

At times, the homework seemed punitive rather than constructive; at the very least it lacked thought. Another assignment I marveled at for its sheer lack of direction was a four-page report on anything in the whole science book. Perhaps it was Alejandro's weak receptive English skills or my expectations for some written explanation of such a report (i.e., some connection to a theme) that made the assignment seem so disintegrated to me.

"You mean she just wants you to pick anything from your science book and do a report on it?" I questioned.

"Yeah, Chris. I think I'm gonna do it on the octopus. I heard from a friend of mine that you could find a lot on the octopus," said Alejandro hopefully. "There's encyclopedias at my *comadre's* [co-mother, close friend, or relative actively involved in the child's life] house. I'm just gonna copy it from there."

We had discussed copying versus reading about a topic and then composing, but copying from reference books seemed to be standard fare in Alejandro's class.

"I know how to do a report, Chris," Alejandro reassured me. I had brought a book on Malcolm X for young readers to the tutoring session, and Alejandro told me he had gotten a good grade on a report he did last year on Malcolm X.

"I even got extra credit for typing it and putting it in a folder," he said. "I'm gonna bring it to show you next week."

Alejandro's main concern about the present report was that it be four pages both sides, handwritten. This was the command he had to fulfill. He had developed a system for stretching out his material to fill as much paper space as he could. He wrote long headings and titles and skipped numerous lines. The spacing between words was more than ample. Clearly, English literacy for Alejandro meant jumping through hoops for Mrs. Wright. Form took precedence over content; writing was pursued only for teacher approval. Any sense of self-satisfaction or creativity for Alejandro was nonexistent. Skill sheets and workbooks dissected language as well and were frequently used to "drill" grammar. Those I saw at our tutoring sessions always struck me as particularly confusing to second language speakers. For example, one format used to drill adverbs and adjectives consisted of giving an incorrect sentence to be rectified. I was sure, however, that sentences like *She worked real hard to become a doctor* and *She became the country's first real qualified female doctor* sounded fine in the nonstandard dialect of English Alejandro and his classmates shared.

So when I began to observe in Mrs. Wright's fourth-floor classroom, I must admit that I entered with some preconceived notions of how she taught and what she taught.

"Alejandro rarely, if ever, volunteers to participate in class," Mrs. Wright informed me when I asked for her permission to observe in the classroom.

"That's okay," I answered. "I need to see him in the context of his classrooms. I'd really appreciate it if I could." It became routine for me to plead with Sorrowful Mother junior high teachers for permission to get into their classrooms. Although I had received the principal's permission to observe in Alejandro's classes earlier in the year, actually setting up times with individual teachers was extremely difficult. I was careful to emphasize my interest in Alejandro and avoid the issue of observing the teacher, which was, of course, a natural byproduct of the close observation I was doing with Alejandro.

It was a cold, still, gray day when I finally entered Mrs. Wright's room. I slipped into a seat in the back and began taking copious notes on the setting in which I found myself. I fear that even my note taking bothered Mrs. Wright. On one occasion when she had students working in groups in the library, she began to clean a cabinet behind me, standing on a chair to do so, and I could not help but feel that she was looking over my shoulder at my notebook.

From the windows of the old fourth-floor classroom that day in Mrs. Wright's room, a panorama of Chicago's west side unfolded. Row after row of brown and red brick bungalows, two- and three-flat buildings, bare winter trees, and puffing smoke stacks made up the horizon. Glimpses of cars, like matchbox toys, could be seen moving up and down the road. A huge billboard dominated the vista. It advertised a quaint "Discount Mall." An adobe-like arch with wrought iron fencing adorned the entrance, creating a very Mexican flavor. In actuality, the "Mall" was a small group of neighborhood stores set back from *la vienteseis* [26th street], called by some *la avenida Mexicana* [Mexican Avenue]. The business pulse of the community is palpable driving down 26th Street. One could easily understand how Latino families in the area could insulate themselves from any need of the English language to conduct the everyday business of their households.

Inside Mrs. Wright's classroom, everything was orderly. Desks were lined into straight rows. There was an old wooden display cabinet filled with nicely arranged shells and wood samples. Each bulletin board was covered with posters or postcards, appropriate sayings, and a few student papers. The displays were linear and neat. In the front corner there was a flag, a clock, a statue of St. Mary, a Bible, a globe—all in perfect order. Next to her own large oak teacher desk was a small student desk where Mrs. Wright neatly stored her books and manuals. Her main desk was immaculate. The supply closet door had a Mexican *sombrero* hanging from the doorknob; there is a statue of Our Lady of Guadalupe. A doily with a vase is centered on a small metal cabinet next to the closet. Nothing was out of place; no papers laid on anyone's desk. Mrs. Wright carefully covered all five maps on her walls with construction paper so that her students can't copy from them on geography quizzes. Everything is under control.

She started the class by collecting homework; she called every "line," one at a time, to bring up their papers, which she stapled immediately, should a student hand in more than one page. This appears to be a familiar routine to the students. Not only does she have a pronounced Australian accent but her choice of vocabulary and some phrases she uses are colloquial as well. Her students are in lines, not rows. She speaks of something being "a little way away," describes things as being "pleasant," asks "has anybody not got their lesson?" Her limited-English-proficient students (all speaking nonstandard English) are actually dealing with a fourth dialect in their lives. Added to Mexican Spanish, American English, and English slang, they cope as well with Australian English. But Mrs. Wright has a rule that she will not repeat things said orally in class. To her, failure to hear what she has said has only one explanation—inattention. Second language needs seem simply not to be entertained or given credibility.

The day I observe in her room, a science lesson on nonrenewable resources is under way. Mrs. Wright is seated at her desk reading to her pupils from the textbook, periodically asking questions as a way to check comprehension. She is a master of the pseudo-question format, eliciting, almost exclusively, one- or two-word answers from her students. In fact, she used a "close format" that morning, as reading teachers would label it, a kind of fill-in-the-blank format done verbally. Students need only supply the correct word as their class participation.

In trying to describe a type of stone to her class, she used examples of some downtown Chicago buildings.

"Who's ever been to the Water Tower? Bloomingdale's a good example of that stone," said Mrs. Wright. The students looked at each other quizzically. "Bloomingdales?" someone repeated. Most of the families of students in her class live in the surrounding Mexican neighborhoods and struggle economically.

She used the Amoco Building as an example of Italian limestone and the climatic problems it faced in Chicago; again, the students aren't familiar with the example she chooses. I couldn't stop thinking how helpful a trip downtown or some pictures of these buildings would be. Or how effective examples of marble and limestone used in their own neighborhood could be.

To her credit, after these two unsuccessful referents she speaks of the value she sees in going to Yellowstone National Park and compares the length of that drive with one to Texas. She thinks aloud in choosing a state familiar to her Mexican-American audience, and says, "Let's see, what would you know that's about that distance." The class responds well to her choice for comparison. Some mention cities they've visited in Texas. I wished she would extend this kind of meaningful connection to the entire lesson.

Mrs. Wright appeared to have a well-established classroom routine. She read or had students read aloud from the textbook, particularly in social studies and science, then she wrote notes from the reading for them to copy. Alejandro and his classmates needed no directions to perform their tasks. The moment Mrs. Wright stood with her papers and mentioned notes, the otherwise silent classroom burst into a shuffle of papers and snaps of looseleaf binder rings. The checking for comprehension continued; the answers were rated aloud: right, wrong, good, bad. "The Federal Reserve System—what is it?" she asks, and a girl answers with a pat, memorized definition. Alejandro never volunteered to answer. I doubt that he comprehends enough English vocabulary to do so with any confidence despite the very short answers that are sought. At times, Mrs. Wright would even give the first part of a word so that students were down to giving half-word answers.

"What was the president's nickname?" Mrs. Wright asked; no one answers. "He became known as the trust———?" To her questioning intonation someone replied "buster!" "Did the Federal Reserve System do business with the public. Yes or no?" Again she posed her questions so that they require a minimum amount of language production. A student answered in one word.

"Right," said the teacher. It was the first example of student participation in the first half of social studies. When working with second language students it is important to give students opportunities to construct extended oral discourse. But Mrs. Wright clearly was concerned with delivering content within a subject area, not with language development. I doubt that she is conscious of the work being done in content area instruction that is language-sensitive for second language students.

Yet Mrs. Wright was organized and prepared. She did cover content. Hers is a traditional teacher-fronted classroom where her role is that of disseminator of knowledge. Her students are passive receptacles, 99% of classroom discourse in the classes I observe is hers. The student role is to be an attentive receptor of lessons. I could see why Sister Eleanor prized her. She knew her subjects, was organized, clean, punctual, rarely absent, and ran a tight ship. She kept those children in line, in order, within a well-defined structure.

At some point during social studies note taking a girl in the front "line" yawned.

"Tired, are you?" Mrs. Wright scowled. "Hum, tired?" she questioned again, sarcastically, then snickered and wrote even faster on the board. The room must be still during lectures and note taking; nothing less is accepted. Mrs. Wright pounced on even the slightest hint of inattention she captured.

I looked at Alejandro during this routine. After copying notes steadily for half of the class he began to gaze out the window. After seeing Mrs. Wright's reaction to the yawn, he began to copy notes steadily again. Tired and bored, I too found it easy to stare out those high, tall windows at the real life outside them. Imagine not comprehending most of the content you are hearing and copying, I thought as I cover a yawn. I was sure Alejandro has no idea of what a trust or a trustbuster is. For religion homework he once had to write a composition on the affective definition of trust and asked for help. I remembered saying that trust meant you could count on someone, like he knew he could always trust in his parents to help him. His face lit up as he internalized the meaning and he said, "Like I can always trust you too, Chris."

In an English composition class, Mrs. Wright delivered a lesson on writing a formal business letter applying for employment and asking for information or complaining about a service. She referred to these as "formal" letters versus the "social" letters they wrote earlier. I found myself constantly doubting that Alejandro comprehended any of these words, which are uncommon to limited-English speakers. In his background of experiences, all letters are uncommon and comprehension of everyday mail is difficult. After writing an example of such a business letter on the board, Mrs. Wright assigned the class a business letter to write for homework. Someone asks about a letter of application.

"At home you can apply for whatever you want to. You could be applying for the position of secretary of the U.N., I don't care," she answers off-handedly, but not maliciously.

"Be sure to use unlined paper, never, ever put this kind of letter on lined paper . . . do not write numerals under one hundred in value, always spell them out . . . be sure to indent and miss a line before a new paragraph . . . don't write 'Dear Sir,' because if it's a woman she won't take kindly to you calling her 'sir.' . . . " The rules went on and on. Form clearly dominated content in this lesson.

A student asked a question after Mrs. Wright explains how to write out an envelope.

"Do we put a stamp on it?" she asked tentatively.

"Don't put a stamp on it; that's a waste. Oh, maybe you could draw one on if you like," answered Mrs. Wright.

What does that say about their work, I wondered. Why couldn't they write an authentic letter to a real organization asking for information of interest to them? Wouldn't that be a way to practice form without ignoring content? Then the students could use a real stamp and receive a bona fide business letter in reply to theirs. These ideas raced through my mind. I found myself wishing I could have organized that lesson.

Although I could not observe her classes as frequently as I had hoped to due to her reluctance to allow me to be there, I believe I saw Mrs. Wright's usual routine. Alejandro told me that when I am not there, Mrs. Wright does most of the textbook reading herself, not calling on students to read as she did when I visited. "She's nicer to us when you come," said Alejandro. Most teachers would be, I think. What I did see firsthand, throughout the entire year, was the curriculum she doled out through homework assignments. It gave me a good understanding of her philosophy of teaching, which is shared by many educators. She accepted the burden of being the disseminator of knowledge; she faithfully covered content. I also saw her routinely about the building, saw her "way" with students. She was guarded; she was in charge; she expected obedience.

Despite the inauthenticity of the work she assigned in her classes and the lack of meaningful educational experiences, as I drove home that day I found myself thinking that many people would see Mrs. Wright as a good teacher. And in some sense she is for she works hard to deliver a kind of schooling she values. In some of my own daughters' traditional Catholic suburban classrooms she would be held in high regard as an organized and competent teacher. Like many teachers I have seen, she has difficulty individualizing, deviating from the program of content she strives to impart, even when significant segments of her student population need something more than textbook coverage. Her language would have been more comprehensible to suburban standard English-speaking students like those filling my children's classrooms. In fact, her dialect probably would enhance her desirability as a faculty member in an affluent suburb. For unlike Mexican Spanish, hers is an esteemed accent in this country.

I, too, could see her in a positive light as a teacher capable of offering an orderly, safe, predictable environment for junior high students in a neighborhood where many students do not receive those basics in their classrooms. I had been prepared to see her only negatively after having seen the curriculum she imposes through homework assignments, her cold manner, and what I perceived as a lack of respect for some students. Yet, in fairness, the teacher I saw was well prepared for the traditional delivery of content and did control her temper while I was present. Although I have serious disagreements with her ways, particularly what I perceive as her total inattention to second language issues, the lack of authenticity and meaning in her curriculum, and the lack of opportunity for student input, and with her stern, insensitive punishments, I cannot overlook the fact that she does have a sanctioned philosophy of education, which she follows conscientiously. It is her way, and in the culture of Sorrowful Mother School, it is accepted and encouraged. In fact, there were some students who, I was told by another staff member, like Mrs. Wright very much. Some girls have even visited her at home. "She is strict, but she's a good teacher," they were reported as saying. However, Alejandro's group, the less successful students in the class, did not share this sentiment.

Alejandro must have been something unnervingly out of order in Mrs. Wright's classroom world. He is a student who struggled in reading, could barely write, laughed at the wrong time, and in general, as Luis Rodriguez wrote of his own comprehension difficulties in school, "mixed up all the words. Screwed up all the songs" (1993, p. 27). Alejandro was punished toward the end of the school year for not wearing his school uniform. He had mixed up the days of the week and thought it was the day of an upcoming field trip, when uniforms were not required. Consequently, on the correct field trip day he had to wear his school uniform for his failure to comprehend the plans. According to Mrs. Wright's way, there is obedience and disobedience, good and bad, right and wrong, and Alejandro usually lined up on the wrong side of most of those distinctions.

"He needs to try harder," Mrs. Wright told Alma when she questioned her son's many failing grades. "He'll be able to graduate, but don't tell him that," added Sister Eleanor. "We have to see that he tries harder." This confused Alma, who wondered what more her son can do. It is a little like asking, in French, an English-speaking first grader, who has not learned to do the basic operations of adding, subtracting, multiplying, and dividing to work harder on some algebraic equations.

Alejandro was hopelessly out of order in Mrs. Wright's neat and orderly world. Yet, he tenaciously hung on, albeit by a thread, to his classroom world. He made sure he had unlined paper for letter writing, completed punishment assignments by writing incomprehensible vocabulary over and over again, copied reports from encyclopedias, heard from his peers "through the grapevine" which topics might satisfy requirements, filled in the blanks of sentences he barely understood, tried to conform to Mrs. Wright's way. He may not have gotten the field trip instructions quite right, but he managed to bring in the permission slip his parents did not comprehend and to make the event, even in the face of the embarrassment of being the only student in uniform. The waters of his educational journey were as rough as those of his parents' first crossing of *la frontera*. Yet, like them, he did not retreat. He may get the words to the songs wrong, but he does not give up on the tune.

"Teacher, What Is Art?"

And so her heart was ready to break once again but then, to her surprise,
each new peril only showed her a deeper mystery in this dream called life,
la vida.

—Rain of Gold, V. Villaseñor

Somewhere along the way, in our travels revolving around her son, Alma
began to call me quite regularly on Sunday nights. Her phone calls were
delightful, very polite, always, as is the traditional Mexican custom,
beginning with inquiries as to the health and general well-being of my
family, and ending with *saludos* [warm wishes] for each and every
member.

"My husband wants you and your family to come to dinner so I
can cook our food for you," she would begin. Enjoying Mexican dishes
was a cultural bridge over which we could join hands and hearts despite our families' language limitations. Mr. and Mrs. Juarez delighted
in seeing my husband and children enjoy their culinary specialties, which
I honestly could never cook as well, or with the same *sabor* [flavor] as
Alma did.

The ostensible reason for the call aside, Alma would then proceed
to tell me that she had been thinking of me a lot and wondering why
I wanted to help her son. "Why am I always so lucky?" she would say.
"The nuns in Mexico just loved Alejandro too. My *comadre* loves him.
She wants him to come over all the time. She treats him to things. She
even offered to take him on a trip to California with her and her family. Why, Christina? Why?"

This became a familiar theme in our conversations and would sur-
face again and again, over the phone, in my car, around her kitchen
table. Despite my attempts to explain my own interest, Alma would
ponder what she considered to be her undeserved good fortune. "You
know, Alejandro was an altar boy in Mexico and the nuns hoped he
would become a *padre* [priest, literally "father"]. But Alejandro told

me that the only kind of *padre* he wanted to become was the kind with children, like his own father." She and her children enjoyed this anecdote immensely, and Alejandro blushed at its retelling.

But Alma truly grappled with this question, and I searched for ways to explain my own motives, which went far beyond that of a researcher. I kept coming back to one basic fact, again and again; he was just such a nice kid, sweet really. What was difficult to translate was my feeling that he had never been given a fair shake, so to speak, by education. I wanted him to experience someone in education who didn't write him off as another deficient minority student hopelessly weak in language skills.

I began to realize over the months that Alma's question was really a rhetorical one to which no specific answer would ever suffice. Periodically she thinks out loud in the form of a question as to why people seem to take an interest in her son. But actually, I think, it is more of a statement of recognition of his "specialness" in her eyes, a wonderful, unexplained quality about a child she has given birth to and nurtured into adolescence that people like. It affirms not only Alejandro but her and her husband as well.

One Sunday evening phone call late in the winter skipped the usual invitations and ponderings, though never the inquiries as to everyone's well-being. "They told Alicia that they want to test her in school," she said. "Alicia is upset; she says they think she's crazy. They said something about a psychological evaluation." The public school had sent some forms to Alma to explain their concern with her daughter's school performance but Alma could not read them. This was left unstated.

I visited Alma and read the forms requesting a psycho-educational evaluation for her oldest daughter. Alicia had been unhappy with her new school, particularly with her new teacher. In the fall she related that her teacher, a middle-aged African-American woman, had the habit of digging her long fingernails into the shoulders of students who weren't reading aloud quickly enough, and sometimes shouting at them. She came home in tears one day because the teacher had dug her nails into her. Mr. Juarez related the story to me when he picked up Alejandro from our after-school tutoring session.

"All the years my children went to Catholic school," he shook his head and pointed to Sorrowful Mother as we stood talking in front of the school, "they never laid a hand on them. I don't like this at all. Alicia was so upset and afraid." She is a very quiet, extremely conscientious girl who struggles with second language issues but had never had any behavior problems in school.

I encouraged Mr. Juarez to speak to the teacher or the principal of the public school. "If it happens again, I will," he said. But he was hesitant to do so immediately. Traditional Mexican parents hold the position of *maestra* [teacher] in very high regard. The teacher is treated with the utmost respect and given complete trust as the educator of their offspring. When the teacher is also a member of a religious community, that respect is amplified. Even with solidly just cause, Mr. Juarez would not rush into a challenge of a teacher's behavior, even a nonreligious teacher.

Alma felt that Alicia was afraid of her teacher because she had never had an African-American in that role before and because of the nail digging. She did, however, believe that Alicia was feeling a little better about things in school lately.

"I'm afraid it's my fault," said Alma. "First, Alejandro has trouble in reading in school, now Alicia. I think it's because I don't have a good memory either and we don't speak English." She began to cry.

"My husband says I worry too much about these things at school. He says I shouldn't get so upset. But I want to know what's wrong, why does this happen with my kids?" Alma knew that her children were well behaved and tried hard in school, especially Alicia, who she worried spent too much time on homework and needed to relax about it.

In Spanish, there really aren't good translations for the labels educators place on students like Alma's. "At risk," "limited English proficient," "learning disabled," "linguistically delayed"—it seemed futile to attempt translations for they would have been only labels without concepts to Alma. And what good do the labels do for a parent anyway, I wondered. What good do they do for the children?

So instead I spoke to her about how difficult it is to be judged academically in a language that is not your native tongue, to have your school performance measured in terms of what mainstream, monolingual English speakers could accomplish. I acknowledged her concern, particularly for Alejandro, who had a weak memory compounded by the strain of second language demands. I ended by saying that I thought of school achievement as just one small aspect in the realm of important things in a child's life—her children were good kids, loving, responsible, thoughtful, resourceful. I thought these qualities were a lot more crucial to life than the ability to get high grades in a school system that never tried to look at their strengths, but only their deficits.

I accompanied Alma to Alicia's staffing. She had been spared this experience with Alejandro, who had been tested privately while at Sorrowful Mother. His evaluation confirmed his deficits, but nothing was done consistently to emphasize his strengths and design an appropriate curriculum. The Juarezes never fully understood the meaning of Alejandro's testing. Now they faced yet another evaluation.

Alma was very nervous as we made our way to the conference room on the school's third floor. I realized how intimidating the entire format is for a parent, especially one who does not speak the same language the school personnel do and has only a second-grade formal education. It was intimidating to me as well—the "experts" clearly were there to tell us what was wrong with the child we represented. We were at their mercy. Within 5 minutes, tears rolled down Alma's face as the bilingual social worker related Alma's concerns that her daughter is too serious and perhaps has had too much responsibility for household tasks because of her own second-shift work schedule. Later she lamented her frankness with the social worker, "I should never have told her so many of my worries," she said.

Basically, the school wanted to label Alicia as learning disabled so that she could receive remedial reading assistance. I objected to the labeling and questioned some of the conclusions I felt were drawn without consideration of second language issues. I asked about ESL classes but was told they were not available. The psychologist who did the testing was not in attendance to answer my inquiries, and we were assured that Alicia would have the L.D. label removed from her files as soon as she improved her reading level.

"This is the only way she can receive any special help," we were told by the coordinator of the staffing. They had to label her in order to get funds for the special programs from government money earmarked for specific labeled populations. Alicia's staffing overran its allotted time, and suddenly we were rushed out of the room. I had the feeling that time for parental questions was not routinely worked into these meetings. The coordinator promised to let us speak to the absent psychologist and said that Alma should have some time to think over everything before signing Alicia into the L.D. program. Within seconds the next apprehensive looking Latino mother was seated where Alma had been and another staffing was under way.

We were never allowed to speak to the psychologist who did Alicia's evaluation, and after more assertions over the phone that Alicia would receive none of the help she needed without the L.D. label, Alma signed the papers. The Latino school social worker also took us aside the day of the staffing and whispered, "This evaluation will make the family eligible for some money from social security. Alicia will be classified as a disabled child. Here's a number to call. You could use the money they give you for tutors or a computer for the kids, anything educational." I wondered what criteria she used for letting parents in on this secret. Alma was interested in the prospect of financial aid; I was just more amazed at the machinations revolving around the staffing process. It was my first experience with one. From the prestaffing where no translator was provided except one district nurse who knew, with poor pronunciation, the Spanish words for childhood diseases but no verbs or grammar to connect them into language, to the hurried formal staffing where pressure was exerted to get this "thing" done and conform to school wishes, I saw huge holes in the process. I wondered what kind of information Alicia's prestaffing would have yielded if I had not been there to re-translate the nurse's pathetic efforts in Spanish. Alma would turn to me after each of the nurse's questions and whisper, "What did she say?" The multidisciplinary team coordinator and other special education and nursing staff consulting on the case were very defensive about any need for translation. All seemed to feel they knew what was best for Alicia and they could do their jobs just fine without knowing her parent's language. Mrs. Juarez's input was one big hole to which only lip-service was provided. At many points, Alma or I had to remind the evaluation team of her daughter's name.

I felt tremendous conflict over counseling Alma through this event. At every point in the process she asked me for my opinion, with total trust. In the end, the carrot of special help for Alicia lured me away from the disdain I had for the entire categorization game involved in special education. Faced with the reality of her need for some kind of consideration, I realized that in the Chicago public school system accepting an L.D. label was the only way she could get anything out of the ordinary. And the ordinary was not working for Alicia.

Before we left Shepherd School the day of the staffing, we stopped in the school office to enroll Alma's children in an after-school program the teacher had recommended. Alma couldn't understand why her children weren't allowed to attend the after-school classes; she had been trying to get them included in this program for weeks. Their participation in it would give Alejandro a chance to get home from Sorrowful Mother by bus to watch the younger children when both she and her husband worked. It would also give them something to do other than watch T.V. all afternoon. After being directed to three different staff members by one of several secretaries who obviously wished we weren't there, we finally found out that the after-school program director needed a written note from the parent requesting the services. This prerequisite could have kept Alma's children out of the program due to her problem with written language. This always was a delicate situation in my relationship with Alma, but I went ahead and asked her if I could write the permission notes for her to sign. She seemed relieved. At times such as these I always remembered her frankness the first day I spoke to her at length as we drove Alejandro to the college for some tests. She hated to have to depend on other people for reading and writing, she said. Yet there were clearly moments in our relationship where my ability to use print could greatly facilitate the help she needed for her children, particularly within the educational system.

Finally, the after-school director asked me to translate for Alma whether she wanted her youngest son enrolled in a "Games" class or an "Art" class. I explained the choice just briefly.

"Um, art, I think," she answered the director hesitantly.

As we walked down the hall, back to the car, Alma turned to me and said, "Teacher, what is art?"

Her choice, I realized, had been one more in opposition to "games," which didn't sound academic enough to her, than in favor of art per se.

I was taken aback by the innocence of her question. A mighty responsibility I thought, to define art! We were passing some bulletin boards displaying paper snowmen, and I explained that art was drawings, paintings, crafts, like those snowmen. Alma murmured a long "oh . . . ," as if she had never connected the word with the concept before. And, I wondered, what sense could she have made of the educational jargon that was tossed about at the staffing 5 minutes earlier, which was so much more intimidating than "art"?

"I think that art would help him more in school, don't you, Christina?"

She seemed almost instinctively to manage to look out for her children, to try to help them to succeed, to make good choices. She would notice this feat herself one day later in the year, when she told me, "I don't know how I do it; I don't understand a lot of English. But when Alejandro is playing music in English with words that aren't good, I just know it and ask him what's going on."

Alejandro laughed, "Yeah, it's true, she does; I don't know how she does it but she always knows if we're trying to get something by her!"

Driving home from the staffing, Alma said to me, "When you have your children you're just so happy, right? Everything is happiness. I remember, my husband and I were so thrilled with our babies. We never thought about the problems that could happen later on. We never even thought about it." She was deep in thought, misty-eyed, laying her most profound realizations in my hands just as she had laid her innocently eloquent question of the essence of art at my feet 10 minutes earlier. I do not take these moments lightly; I cradle them in my heart, grateful that a sister human being has entrusted them to me, has proffered them so sweetly, so genuinely, into the arms of my consideration.

I have realized that Alma will prevail despite the jargon of special education, the bureaucracy of the Chicago public school system, her difficulties with English, and a vocabulary worlds apart from her own experiences in Michoacán. For her, life is often a mystery; she is accustomed to uncertainty.

"If you take off the old buds, the roses will bloom again. An old woman in my village taught me that and I always had the fullest rose bushes around. I don't know for sure, but they might even grow again next year," she told me one day in my backyard. Although I didn't know enough to remove the old blooms, I knew rose bushes were perennials and would, barring disaster, grow again after winter. Yet, to Alma, it seemed a wondrous unpredictable possibility rather than a fact learned in a science class or gardening book. *La vida* [life], replete with its mysteries and perils, could alter her dreams but never defeat her hope.

"I'm Your Best Friend"

My Papa, his thick hands and thick shoes, who wakes up tired in the dark, who combs his hair with water, drinks his coffee, and is gone before we wake, today is sitting on my bed.

And I think if my own Papa died what would I do. I hold my Papa in my arms. I hold and hold and hold him.

—*The House on Mango Street*, S. Cisneros

Mr. Juarez is a hard-working, quiet, and serious man. Mrs. Juarez is energetic, talkative, and fun-loving. They complement each other well. I believe that their intensity best comprises their common ground. Alma pursues an idea, follows a lead, watches out for her children aggressively. Mr. Juarez works unobtrusively and tirelessly. When I visit their home, Alma chats and runs the show, while Mr. Juarez quietly and constantly toils in the background. He practically runs from chore to chore as he does from job to job. While doing so he is very serious, as if impending disaster is just around the corner. Both he and his wife approach their lots in life with strong faith in God, frequently verbalizing it as a part of their everyday conversation. During his life, Mr. Juarez has tended pigs, worked in construction, painted, washed dishes, dug ditches, made ice cream, and sold tacos in order to scratch out a living. In *Always Running* (1993), Luis Rodriguez wrote that Mexican men will do anything to earn a living, anything. No job is too menial. Alejandro's father certainly bears out that observation. For him, there is dignity in work, any work.

I have found that over the months I've come to know Alma and her husband I do not feel comfortable addressing Mr. Juarez as Alejandro. Even as I write, I feel compelled to name him with the title Mr.—*Señor*. It is not because I feel any distancing or coldness from him, but rather because of the respect I feel for this parent, this fellow human being whose road is a difficult one. Yet, he meets his challenges head-on, with great clearness of purpose and gravity. His demeanor beckons esteem; he is direct, honest, and soberly productive.

59

Alma, on the other hand, solicits opinions, nudges, and befriends with more ease. She is frequently Mr. Juarez's spokesperson. "My husband wants to stop by . . . my husband wants you to talk to Alejandro," Alma often will say. It is as if he needs her to test the waters, to set the stage, to be sure he is not doing something out of line, for he deeply respects the profession of teaching.

Mr. Juarez contradicts the stereotypical Latino "macho" image and is an active, concerned, and loving father. He is the glue that keeps the household together—serving food Alma leaves for them while she works, cleaning tables, mopping floors, tidying the toys and trappings of five children, guiding them all through a life he perceives as perilous. And always, consistently, thanking God aloud for the help they receive. Alma is the heartbeat of this home—the quintessential mother whom all look to for direction and concern. Keenly aware of her husband's earnest and preoccupied nature, she worries for his health and the visible fatigue he experiences from 16- to 18-hour double work shifts, 6 days a week. She mentions repeatedly that her family and friends tell her what a good husband she has.

"I may have other troubles but I know that I was lucky to find the husband I have," she told me. "He and Alejandro, Jr. clean the whole house; I really don't have to do it. They do it better than I could." More important, though, is her realization that he truly, without doubt or reservation, loves her.

It is not only the physical help he provides in the household that she acknowledges but also his deep commitment to providing for her and their children. Employment is never taken for granted in their home. Mr. Juarez has experienced extended unemployment from a construction company he worked for over the past 8 years. During a year without work, Alma's pay supported them, just barely. Alejandro, Sr. was no stranger to the need for work, as that was the problem that precipitated his immigration from Mexico. He eventually made the difficult decision to find a new, lower paying but steady job rather than wait and hope that the construction business would pick up again and that he would be called back to work. His unemployment was making him physically ill, so great was his concern over the lack of family income. The educational literature often refers to the low socioeconomic status of urban minority families. I once read an article that phrased the problem as "low or threatened income" and felt that the phrase better described the plight of many urban Latino families I had seen. In the case of Mr. Juarez in particular, I believe that "threatened" is precisely the word to describe his experience and his response to employment concerns. It is a feeling that pervades the household, a constant fear of the loss of income and concomitant loss of health insurance.

Alejandro and his siblings adore Mr. Juarez. Whenever he is home they are near him. Alma laughs that he wants the whole family with him all the time, even when she wants him to run an errand quickly by himself. Although they grumble about his insistence on neatness in the house, his position as the beloved, reliable patriarch is totally embraced. Alejandro works at his father's side, fully aware of the complete commitment to him this man—small in stature, yet large in character—possesses. And Mr. Juarez keeps Alejandro at his side, supremely aware of the danger of gang involvement for a Mexican-American boy of his age, determined to protect and provide for his son, unlike his own parents who were unable to do so for him.

During the Christmas break from school my daughters and I visited the Juarez's home one evening while Alma was at work. Mr. Juarez was in charge that evening and took over the role of food preparer and converser that is typically Alma's. He struggled to produce different meals for the young children and the adults but managed to serve everyone. I complimented him on his choice of food, pizza, for all of our children, which everyone enjoyed, unlike the dinner I had prepared a couple of weeks earlier. They all laughed and began making apologies once again about spaghetti and their lack of familiarity with *gringo* [North American, Caucasian] foods in general. As he worked in the kitchen, he spoke of his concern for Alejandro at school, his fear that Alejandro would get involved with kids who were "bad."

"Some of the boys in my class are drinking, you know, liquor, Tequilla, in the washroom during school. Then they eat lemons to kill the smell," Alejandro, Jr. explained. Mr. Juarez was so afraid that his son would be influenced by these youngsters that he refused to let Alejandro go on an ice-skating trip that some of the teachers arranged during the holidays. Alejandro told me of the event at that Christmas visit and of his father's reluctance to give him permission to attend it. I felt an unspoken request for intercession. Alejandro teased as he cajoled his father into reconsidering the trip. He is so much like his mother in that way. Rather than confrontation, they both choose a more gentle approach, couching their concerns in jokes. "He wants me to stay in this house all the time," he laughed. "I tell him, 'It's boring!'"

I did intercede and say that I thought supervised trips like this were just great for junior high kids. Alejandro smiled widely. "I just wanna be with my friends," he said and spoke of being stuck babysitting in the house throughout the entire holiday break.

Mr. Juarez said to me, "I told him [Alejandro], you don't need friends from school; I'm your best friend." I smiled at his refusal to budge on the issue of friends but realized that he was serious. He truly felt, he explained, that he could take Alejandro to places and do things with him and that he should feel no need to get involved with his peers.

"I don't want him hanging around with those kids from school; they're bad," he said as he folded his arms and shook his head. This was his response to the realities of urban life for a Latino adolescent male. Alma and her husband united in their dedication to shielding their oldest son from what they clearly saw as a dangerous influence— peers. Like the encircled carts of a wagon train, their strategy was to enfold him within their flock, their extended family, and ward off the dangers of the outside world. Alejandro is well-accepted by his peers at school and often pursued by the girls in his class, who find him very handsome despite his academic problems. He is quite good at covering up his weaknesses—he rarely volunteers answers at school, hands in assignments conscientiously, pitches in on activities he feels confident in, especially clean up tasks, lettering, and drawing. For example, Alejandro has great difficulty saying letter names, a task most first graders can do. He confuses English and Spanish vowel names and reverses *b*'s and *d*'s, and mixes up other letters too. Yet, in playing a computer game with his partners in school he found a joking way to get around helping with multiple choice letter answers. He would point to the letter on the screen that he wanted his partners to type in, holding his head excitedly, speaking alternately in English and Spanish, pretending to be so excited that he just couldn't say the answers. Sometimes his partners became frustrated with his slow decoding of answer choices, but Alejandro managed to laugh his way through the timed games, occasionally contributing some correct answers and just being pleasantly involved in the activity, enjoying it. He made it easy for the kids to like him even if he wasn't the best computer partner to have. Although his academic problems are severe, he has found ways to cope in front of his friends.

I saw that in class he was a follower. He thoroughly enjoyed the mischief some of his peers got into, although he did not actively participate in it.

When I observed him working in small groups in social studies, computer, and religion classes, I saw a side of him with which I was unfamiliar. Perhaps it was something his parents sensed that I did not. Alejandro sought out the kids who clowned around in class. He did not project the image of a struggling but serious student, which I had seen in our tutoring sessions and in his remedial reading class consisting of just him and one other student. When in a large group, he definitely drifted toward fun, which usually meant toward the kids who were breaking rules and distracting the class.

Once when I was observing classes, Alejandro's religion teacher at *Sorrowful Mother*, a young woman, mentioned that she could change her plans for small group work to more of a lecture class because I was observing. I encouraged her not to change plans because I really wanted to see Alejandro in an authentic situation with his classmates. I mentioned how I was seeing a side of him I hadn't seen before in our one-to-one work.

"Yeah," she said. "When he works in a small group he's kind of, well, goofy." I was surprised by her frankness and lack of an attempt to find a more professional word to describe a student's behavior. She quickly explained that he wasn't a behavior problem but rather that he got distracted by those who were and openly enjoyed them. I talked to Alejandro about the image that his laughing and fooling around with his peers when they broke into small groups could give to a teacher. I began to understand, perhaps, why Mrs. Wright did not see him as a student with genuine academic needs.

"I try not to laugh," Alejandro said. "But they make me smile; a smile just comes to my face," he said. Alejandro often used passive verb forms, which made him the receiver of actions rather than the perpetrator of them. I felt conflicted; I wanted to observe what actually happened in his school world yet wanted to participate, particularly if I felt I could help Alejandro. I spoke to him on just a few more occasions about his demeanor and his need to do anything he could to project a desire to work hard in school. Soon after those talks, I decided to back off from commenting on his reactions to his peers. When his face dropped as I entered class to observe and I saw him struggle to be almost sullen, I felt I was losing something authentic. I searched, instead, for moments to praise, such as those when I saw him try to voluntarily participate in class, obviously because I was there.

During the Easter break, I received an early morning call from Alma. She and her husband just could not decide whether to allow Alejandro to go to the library in downtown Chicago with some of his friends. What did I think, they wanted to know. Their struggle with his peer relationships is an ongoing one. I am known among my own suburban female-peers as a very protective parent. This was no easy question for a person who sees many situations as fraught with danger for children. But I did encourage Alma to give Alejandro a specific time limit and allow him to go to the Harold Washington Library by train with two other boys from class whom I recognized as responsible students. I called that evening to see how things went, and Alejandro

described it as the best day of his Easter break. Later that week he wrote
this journal entry:

April 1993

My spring Becation

On my spring becation it was kind of boring. Because I dirent
have anything to do. But one day was fun it was on a Wednesday becaus we went on the train. We went to the libery some of
us found what we were looking for, Becaus some of then were
hard to find. From the rest of teh weak I dirent go nowere so I
stood home for the rest of the days.

Alejandro Juarez, Jr.

Alma told me she knew that her husband really believed in being
Alejandro's best friend. "He's told me the same thing he said to you,"
she recalled. Despite the success of their son's small trip to the library,
time for peers would remain an uphill battle for Alejandro. Although I
recognize the importance of friendships for him, I cannot help but
admire this pensive, family-centered young father who insists that he
can fill the role of both parent and friend in order to protect his son
from the real dangers of urban neighborhoods. Alejandro is not going
to step out of his school doors and find Dick and Jane characters to
befriend him. He has related his knowledge of alcohol and drug use to
me and to his parents, has alluded disparagingly to sexual behavior by
some of his classmates, has talked about parties where soft drinks are
laced with narcotics and given to unknowing consumers. This activity
is so prevalent in his neighborhood that family and close friends have
repeatedly warned him never to accept an opened pop can for a drink.

In their new Brighton Park neighborhood, Alejandro and his
younger brother and small cousins have been confronted by Chicago
police detectives while playing basketball in their own alleyway.

"My little cousin from Mexico was wearing his cap backwards, you
know," Alejandro told me on one of our summer mini-field trips to a
downtown museum. "The detectives came and started yelling at him
because of his hat. I told them we don't know nothin' about those signs
with the hats, we're just playing ball."

"Were you sure they were really detectives?" I asked.

"Oh, yeah," answered Alejandro. "They have those special blue
cars and they got patches on their shirts. Did you know those detectives, they got those sticks like the cops, only skinnier, and they're allowed to hit you with them. They were really rough with us; they put
a big light on us."

"Oh, it was at night?" I asked.

"Yeah, like around 8:20," he answered. "They told us they were gonna take us to jail, even the little kids, if they saw us with hats on again. They pushed my cousin's hat. They weren't nice. They got mad at my cousin because he spoke Spanish; you know, he doesn't know any English yet. He just got here from Mexico."

"I bet you were scared, Alejandro," I said, remembering the high hopes his parents had for this new neighborhood.

"No, not really. I knew I didn't do nothin' wrong. There's lots of cops around this neighborhood and they stop Mexican kids all the time. They stopped me in the park one day. Some of them talk to you nice, but some are mean. But I don't wear hats, I don't even like them. I just never wear hats. You know, Chris, that's why sometimes I just prefer to stay at home, inside, because of the cops. The other day my father and I saw them chasing two kids down our block."

It's very difficult for a father raised on a ranch in rural Mexico to see his son face the harsh realities of urban neighborhoods of the west side of Chicago. It's a heavy burden that Mr. Juarez takes in deadly seriousness, to try to shield his son from the very real dangers that exist outside his own front door. Although I chuckled when I first heard him say it, Mr. Juarez's assertion, "*I'll* be your best friend," doesn't sound so far-fetched to me any more.

Rusted Wires

I always cry when nuns yell at me, even if they're not yelling.
—*The House on Mango Street*, S. Cisneros

Late in January, Alejandro mentioned to me as we drove home from tutoring that he had received his report card. As I look back on this year I realize that our best conversations have taken place in my car.

"How did you do?" I asked hopefully. The answer was disheartening. All F's and one D in religion.

"I had a B in religion; then Mrs. Wright called me and another boy to her desk and asked for the report cards. She changed my B to a D."

"Did you ask her why? Was it a mistake or what?" I asked.

"No. No, Chris. I didn't ask. I don't know what happened."

I couldn't understand how he could have failed almost everything except physical education. We had been working so hard at his tutoring sessions, which were being dedicated more and more exclusively to his homework needs. Just a few weeks earlier, Mrs. Wright had indicated to Alejandro that his grades were improving. Alejandro was all smiles the day he related that good news to me.

"My mother is real upset. She doesn't give my report card to my father yet to sign because he's at work so much." Mr. Juarez was still employed by a McCormick Place restaurant where he had worked during the holiday season. He had only about an hour between his morning and evening shifts, and Alma was already at her evening 10-hour shift when he had his short break.

"My mother is mad at Mrs. Wright because she said I was doin' better. She doesn't think she likes me," related Alejandro.

I was upset too. I had consistently offered to provide help through the college's tutoring programs in laying out a curriculum for Alejandro. His sixth-grade homeroom teacher had met with me about his studies 2 years earlier and had tried to develop a feasible curriculum for him. But neither Mrs. Wright nor his other teachers in eighth grade had made an attempt to individualize Alejandro's work and recognize his special needs. Only Ms. Gonzalez, his remedial reading teacher who was a recent graduate of a special education program, made any attempt to design a relevant curriculum for him. But she was permitted by Sister Eleanor to work with him only 50 minutes a week and felt that her efforts were practically futile, given their time constraints.

I spoke to Alma that day. She acknowledged that her son had problems in school but felt upset that the teacher had never indicated to her or Alejandro in their conversations before the report card that his work was so poor that he would fail every major subject. Although he had problems with low grades in preceding years, never had he received so many that were so low.

"Ms. Gonzalez was the only teacher who wrote something good about Alejandro. She said he was improving in reading. And my *comadre* [who works as a volunteer teacher aide in Sorrowful Mother] said she thinks Alejandro's reading is getting much better too. She reads with him in school and helps him after school at her home too. I don't understand it," Alma told me.

"I've seen an improvement in his reading too, Alma," I said. "I don't understand how Mrs. Wright could miss it. He's really able to read so much better than he did last year. I think you should talk to Mrs. Wright and ask her if she thinks Alejandro is going to graduate. I don't know what they're planning to do, but with these grades they could keep him back." Alma and her husband were so reluctant to question teachers that I felt I had to suggest some intervention.

Alma said she would talk to her husband about it that night. "He's going to be so disappointed, and Alejandro is so upset and sad. He says he really tries his best and I think Mrs. Wright just doesn't like him," she hesitated to finish her thought. "I think, you know, I think, well maybe she really doesn't like to work with Latinos. I don't know."

Alejandro's parents had already decided that they could not afford to send him to parochial high school. Alma had heard of a good technical high school not far from their neighborhood, a magnet school in the Chicago public school system. She had asked me to look into it and help them find out if Alejandro could get accepted there. Although I had been investigating private high schools with special programs and possible financial aid, I wanted to be open to Alma's input and so began to find out about Crown High School. I was told by one of their counselors that they might accept a student as weak as Alejandro only if I wrote and explained that there had been no room for him at his neighborhood public school and that the parochial school had no special program for him. But *all* failing grades would definitely be an obstacle even to that special consideration. This situation made Alejandro's report card an even greater disappointment for him, and his family feared seeing him go to their neighborhood public school, which had a bad reputation for gang problems.

Although it was boldly intrusive of me, I was so frustrated with Mrs. Wright's attitude toward Alejandro and her lack of sensitivity to second language needs and literacy issues, I asked Alejandro how he would feel about switching to a school with an eighth-grade teacher who would work with him to find a way to improve his school performance. I knew the principal and teachers well at a nearby parochial school where Latino students were approached much differently than they were at Sorrowful Mother. "I want you to experience a compassionate teacher, Alejandro, even if only for half of the year. Six months is a long time to put up with the punishments you keep receiving," I told him. "I know the teacher at St. Charles will try to work with you and find help for you instead of getting mad at you." The punishments for poor memorization just kept coming from Mrs. Wright, the berating of students continued—according to Alejandro. I felt that it was doing far more than academic damage to leave Alejandro in her classroom.

"Are there friends in your class that you'd feel bad to leave?" I asked Alejandro.

"No, Chris. I don't really have anybody that I'd feel bad about," he answered. "I really don't," he insisted as we continued to talk.

"I know you're nervous about this idea. But if your parents agree, Alejandro, why don't you just visit St. Charles's eighth grade for a day and see how you feel?" I suggested.

I spoke to Alma again and she was very interested in the idea of a different, more responsive teacher for her son. I had spoken to St. Charles's principal and also explained to Alma that they were willing to accept him and that they were strongly against retaining students because of English language weaknesses. There he would receive remedial reading daily and would take part in ESL classes in school and after school, if he liked.

"I know our eighth-grade teacher will take him in," said Sister Faith. "She and I have this 'thing' about saving kids from oppressive situations. We took in an eighth-grade boy earlier this year and he's doing just fine now. He was labeled an insolvable behavior problem in another school and he's doing wonderfully here. The kids have accepted him and Mary [the eighth-grade teacher] is really pleased with his work."

But Alma was afraid of Sister Eleanor's reaction to the switch and knew that Alejandro was very shy about meeting a new class.

"I think I'll make an appointment to see Sister Eleanor first," she said.

I thought that was a good idea and I encouraged Alma to ask about the issue of retention and get a specific answer as to whether her son was in danger of failing eighth grade. I was disappointed in what I saw as the loss of the possibility of a positive educational experience for Alejandro and wished I had thought of St. Charles when Shepherd School's eighth grade could not accept him. But I had made the suggestion and wanted to give the Juarezes the freedom to make their own decisions.

After several tries, Alma finally saw Sister Eleanor and Mrs. Wright and asked about Alejandro's chances of graduating. She was told that he would be able to graduate, but that she should not tell him that. "*La Maestra* [Mrs. Wright] said he just needed to try harder, Christina. But you know, she never looked at me when she spoke. She never ever looked me in the face. She just looked toward Sister Eleanor." Alma repeated her observation several times in our conversation and how uncomfortable she felt with Mrs. Wright.

"Please don't tell Alejandro they said he would graduate. Sister Eleanor told us not to, and my husband and I are just going to talk to Alejandro about trying harder. We won't tell him about graduating. She said not to," Alma told me.

Despite the bona fide problems they perceived with their son's treatment in Sorrowful Mother, the Juarezes would not disobey a religious educator's directive. To do so would have been unacceptable for these traditionally raised Mexican Catholic parents.

Almost 2 weeks passed with no mention of leaving Sorrowful Mother. Then, to my surprise, Alejandro called me one Sunday evening and asked to go to St. Charles to spend the day. I asked him if he was sure about doing it and if his parents agreed and he said yes. I didn't know if something happened in Mrs. Wright's room to precipitate his decision, nor did Alma, but I knew that this was a big step for a shy boy like Alejandro. Alma was hopeful and said her husband was too. She said, "We told him it was up to him. We were surprised too, but he wants to try it."

I set up the visitation for that Tuesday and picked Alejandro up early in the morning, driving him to St. Charles myself. He was not a stranger to the school building, for he had attended ESL classes there for the past two summers. That was one of the reasons St. Charles occurred to me, since it was not a totally alien alternative for Alejandro. In fact, his summer ESL class had been held in St. Charles's eighth-grade room, a nontraditional classroom with couches arranged in a reading corner, a small kitchen, and desks set up as a circular group table. It was a very different environment for learning than the perfectly straight "lines" of desks in Mrs. Wright's room with the carefully covered up maps.

Alejandro was quiet and nervous in the car. We stopped at a Burger King for some lunch for him to bring to St. Charles because I had forgotten to tell him to bring one.

"Are you going to leave me there all day?" he almost gasped.

"Well, I planned to, Alejandro. I have some meetings at work and I planned to come back for you at 2:30," I answered. "You'll be fine," I assured him. "Sister Faith [whom he had met] told me that the kids and the eighth-grade teacher were all ready for your visit and looking forward to it."

"Okay, Chris. But it would be okay if you want to come early for me," he said.

As I walked out of St. Charles's eighth-grade classroom after introducing him to Mary, the teacher, I felt oddly like I remembered feeling leaving my oldest daughter for her very first day of school. Mary had been wonderful and broke the ice by saying jokingly, "Don't worry, Alejandro, your hair looks great and you'll do just fine." Hair was a big concern to Alejandro and his classmates; Alma often teased him about the time and effort he put into combing it. Mary had arranged a buddy for Alejandro, who came right up to him and began to show him around the room and introduce him to the other students. I left knowing he was in good hands, although it was hard to go.

Throughout the day I wondered how he was faring and I did arrive a little early to pick him up.

"He sure looked like he was enjoying himself at lunch," Sister Faith assured me as she met me in the hallway. When I walked into the eighth-grade classroom, Alejandro looked happy and content, seated in the middle of the group table chatting with some boys as if they were old classmates.

"Was everything okay?" I asked him as he noticed me and walked over to the doorway.

"It was fine, Chris," he laughed. "They were so nice. The teacher even heated my lunch from Burger King in a microwave because she said she didn't want me to have to eat cold hamburgers!"

As we drove out of the St. Charles parking lot, the kids from eighth grade spotted us as they were leaving the building. They called to Alejandro and said good-bye.

"Are you coming back?" a couple of boys shouted when Alejandro rolled down the car window as we stopped for the crossing guard. "Don't forget about the basketball game. We want you to play."

By this point there were at least half a dozen kids waving and calling to him. Alejandro just laughed in amazement. "They want me to join their basketball team," he explained, "they have a game on Thursday."

"Are you coming back tomorrow?" his buddy asked as we stopped before turning the corner.

"I don't know," answered Alejandro grinning.

"Hey, man, I hope so," said the boy.

"Well, it sure seems like they liked you, Alejandro," I said as we drove away.

"Yeah. They're really nice. They're nicer than the kids in my class."

"Well, how did you like it?" I was dying to hear his reaction.

"It was nice, Chris. I think their math is easier," he answered. But he didn't share anything much more specific with me. He kept repeating, "I liked it. It was nice." He was in an upbeat mood, and I had learned that verbalizing feelings was not something that came easily or quickly for him.

I felt strangely like a criminal when I drove past Sorrowful Mother to the *comadre's* house where his dad was going to pick him up later. Alejandro and his parents did not want to let anyone at Sorrowful Mother know about the possibility of his transfer. We had all agreed to that secrecy until a final decision was made. Alejandro felt odd, too. The specter of Sister Eleanor's fury loomed on the horizon for all of us. We knew that she would be upset with any hint of dissatisfaction with her school. And Alma was particularly concerned with protecting me from Sister Eleanor.

"This will be our decision, my husband and I. I don't even want to mention your name if we decide to move him. I don't want to cause any trouble for you," asserted Alma.

When I confided in Sister Faith, a friend for many years, my own fear of dealing with Sister Eleanor, she was amazed.

"I'm sorry a principal in our own area brings about that reaction. It just shouldn't be," she thought aloud in little more than a whisper.

"I don't want to put you in an awkward position, either," I told Faith. "I know you have to meet with her periodically at west side school meetings."

"Chris, I'm not afraid of Eleanor. I can handle it," Faith reassured me. I had been confiding in her my concerns about the kind of education and treatment Alejandro was receiving all year and she felt that I should have been more assertive about the teacher behavior I was observing, particularly the alleged shoving reported by Alejandro.

"The Archdiocese is very clear on absolutely forbidding any kind of physical aggression in the schools," Faith had told me. "We receive written guidelines and advisories about it all the time."

But I knew that Mrs. Wright was a favorite of Sister Eleanor and that the principal would never accept any criticism of her. I wrestled with this issue all through the year but decided that, particularly because most of the incidents were only related to me by Alejandro (although verified by peers), I would keep it to myself. I feared that Sister Eleanor would cut off any opportunity to work with Alejandro through tutoring or the ESL program if I was critical of anything at Sorrowful Mother. To this day I question my decision. But I am quite sure that to have voiced disapproval of Mrs. Wright's way would have served only to allay my conscience, not to improve the situation for Alejandro or the other limited-English-proficient students in the ESL program. I had seen Eleanor bristle over the years when I or an ESL teacher even mentioned to her that children missed ESL sessions because some teachers just decided not to send them. I could only imagine her reaction to a more serious complaint.

Alma called and told me how much Alejandro had liked St. Charles. "You know what he said, Christina? He said it was more like the schools in Mexico. He said everyone was so friendly, more like a community." She used that word, *community*, to describe her son's reaction.

I was so happy to hear that. Both Alma and I took that comment as a great and positive compliment to St. Charles.

Alma and her husband decided to transfer Alejandro. They wanted to know if the tuition was similar to Sorrowful Mother's, and once those questions were settled, Alma said she would meet with Sister Eleanor. I suggested that both she and her husband meet with Eleanor and Alma agreed to discuss it with Alejandro, Sr. Again she told me that this was their decision and that she would not mention at all that the visit was my suggestion. Alma was convinced that Sister Eleanor would cause problems for me and she knew that I already had problems at the college with a new administrator determined to cut costs.

So Alma requested an appointment with the principal. It took several attempts but she finally was given an audience. It happened to be on a morning when I was in the building, observing in Mrs. Wright's social studies class. The students worked on timelines in small groups, the first such activity I had been able to observe Mrs. Wright conduct, and they periodically went to the office to xerox pictures for their project.

"Alejandro," a friend whispered. "Your mother's in Sister Eleanor's office. How come?"

Alejandro just shrugged his shoulders and kept on working. I continued observing but thinking of poor Alma, who feared this meeting so very much. Eleanor was the only nun I knew who still wore the habit and a modified veil. A tall woman in build, her stature alone was imposing. My own children, upon meeting her one day, told me later that they weren't sure why, but she scared them somehow.

"I can do it, Christina," Alma had told me earlier. "I can meet with Sister Eleanor myself. My husband can't take off from work. But I can do it. I don't know, maybe I'm crazy. But I just go ahead and make myself do something like this. He's our son and we can make this decision," she told me.

When I left the school at lunchtime, there was no sign of Alma or Sister Eleanor. As soon as I got home, the phone rang. It was Alma.

"Oh, Christina, I met with Sister Eleanor, it was terrible. She yelled at me. Her face was bright red. I have such a headache! But I didn't let myself cry in front of her." My heart sank.

"She told me that she wouldn't release his school records and that if he transferred this late in the year he couldn't graduate. I told her that Alejandro's getting stomach pains. He's so tense about school. I told her how he's on medicine for it."

"What did she say?" I asked.

"She called Mrs. Wright into her office and asked her if Alejandro looked nervous at all in class and she said no. Then she told me that it was ridiculous to say that school was making him nervous. I told her that my sister-in-law lives near St. Charles and that Alejandro wouldn't have to take the bus home all the time if he went there, especially in the cold and snow. He could stay with his aunt sometimes. She just kept saying, 'Where did you get this idea? Why do you want to transfer him?' I never mentioned you or the English classes. This was our decision, I kept telling her that. Oh, she was very ugly with me, *muy fea*. But at least I didn't cry."

"I'm so sorry, Alma. I never wanted this to happen. But you know, she can't refuse to send out his records or stop his graduation. That's just not true," I told her.

"I'm afraid of her, Christina. I have such a headache. I'm going to talk to my husband tonight but I don't think we're going to transfer him. She even said she already ordered his cap and gown. I'm afraid of all the trouble she could cause," said Alma sadly. I could hear in her voice that she was shaken. Alma reminded me again, "Christina, at least I can say I didn't break down and cry; I just wouldn't.

"She said she's going to talk to Alejandro, too. She wants to know where he got this idea. I told her it was my idea. Oh, she was not nice at all. And you know what got me even more upset? After Sister Eleanor left, the secretary joined in and said to me, 'You know, if your son's a bad student, switching schools isn't going to change anything!' I told

her that I knew my son wasn't the strongest student, I knew he had
some problems, but he's not a bad boy. She had no right to say anything like that; I didn't like that at all."

Although I had feared Eleanor's reaction, I never thought that she
would be so vehemently aggressive with Alma. Sister Faith had reassured me several times that this was a feasible switch and that no principal should intimidate parents or refuse to accept their decision about
their own child, not even a nun.

I spoke with Alejandro later that day. Eleanor never confronted
him with her inquisition and was at an important meeting, he had heard.
Alejandro adjusted quite easily to remaining at Sorrowful Mother despite the problems with his homeroom teacher. His attitude displayed
the same kind of resignation of which his mother was capable. He could
take it. He not only could do what had to be done but could find something positive to keep him operating. He, too, would not break down.
Alejandro said that he *did* like his school; he felt okay about being there
even after seeing a new world at St. Charles.

I remembered how good I felt driving home on the day of
Alejandro's visit to St. Charles. I had felt for months that the situation
was futile with Mrs. Wright and that, finally, I could do something for
Alejandro that would have a real impact on his education. He would
work with a teacher who respected his culture, recognized his needs,
within a curriculum that emphasized an integrated approach to literacy
and learning. I recalled feeling as if a great weight had been lifted off
my shoulders as a sunny, late winter, snow-melting breeze blew in my
open car windows as I drove home.

After my conversation with Alma, everything seemed bleak and
stifled once again. Although I reassured her and her husband that
Eleanor's threats were actually illegal (I had checked with Sister Faith),
the Juarezes crumbled under Sister Eleanor's forceful disapproval.
Alma's one small triumph was that she maintained her composure.

I once read a Chinese tale of a man who had been imprisoned for
decades. From the shop floor where he was assigned to work he had
gleaned tiny bits of glittering wire, which he put inside a bottle to mark
the passage of time. When he was finally freed, the bottle was the only
possession he had to take with him. Once home, he found himself ris-
ing and sleeping the exact hours he had in prison, even pacing the same-
sized space of his long confinement. One day, in a desperate effort to
break out of his routine, he decided to smash the bottle and count the
pieces of wire. As the broken glass fell around his feet, he wept when
he saw that his collection, after so many years, had rusted into a solid

figure taking the shape of the bottle (Bao Lord, 1990). It reminded me of Alma and Alejandro's dilemma with Sister Eleanor.

A fearful respect for religious educators and clergy is so ingrained in the Mexican culture that I realized it was asking too much of the Juarezes to break the mold of their oppression. Although they made a valiant attempt, the wires of their own historical, social, and cultural experiences were too melded to break free, as were the rusty and coiled wires of the Chinese prisoner. I see my own rusted wires too; I am ashamed to say how I, too, was intimidated by this nun. Although I remembered no one ever directly instructing me to be submissive to these dark garbed women whose faces were framed in white starched wimples, as I thought back to my own childhood experiences, an aura of mystery and an unstated mandate for obedience always surrounded them.

It is with great melancholy that I remember this second failed attempt to move Alejandro out of Sorrowful Mother—not only because it did not succeed but because I am sure that I was culturally insensitive in my expectations of Alma and her husband. Sister Faith, and the few other professional educators I consulted with during this event, assure me that it is Sister Eleanor who should feel remorseful for her poor treatment of a parent, which was far outside the boundaries of behavior one would expect of a principal in this day and age. I am quite sure that Eleanor justified her course of action as being in the student's best interest. Why leave a school, which in her eyes was offering a solid education, half way through eighth grade, the final year? This was incomprehensible and unacceptable to her. Her behavior with Alma, the shouting, the anger—I doubt that it occurred to Eleanor that this uneducated mother deserved her respectful treatment. I still feel bad about the whole incident and, being Catholic myself, feel ashamed that people are treated this way by members of a faith tradition I follow. I am thankful that there is a Sister Faith to counteract what I witnessed in Eleanor, although I am also aware that for Alma there is not such a positive figure. The rusted wires of her oppression remain intact and gnarled.

Shortly after this entire turn of events, less than 2 weeks later, Sister Eleanor was informed by the Archdiocese that she had been relieved of her position and that a new principal would be hired for Sorrowful Mother. It was time for some changes, she was told. Although not advantageous in timing for Alejandro, I couldn't help but think that there was, perhaps, some element of poetic justice in this decision.

Religion Their Way

I grew up a Catholic at home and at school, in private and in public. My mother and father were deeply pious *católicos;* all my relatives were Catholic. . . . When all else was different for me between the two worlds of my life, the Church provided an essential link.

—*Hunger of Memory,* R. Rodriguez

Alejandro occasionally mentioned Mrs. Sommerday. He liked her and he liked her religion classes. When he saw her in the hallways his face lit into a smile and he would attempt a joking remark. I wanted to meet this teacher and see her class but it took me a while to contact her because Alejandro had a problem pronouncing her name and remembering the hour of her class. Finally I deciphered his interpretation of her name and met this personable, young teacher. She seemed very open and frank and didn't try to keep me from visiting her room—a welcomed change of pace for me at Sorrowful Mother.

Mrs. Sommerday's classes were loosely organized, the students sat in groups of four or five, talking often was permitted, desks were joined into tables. Lots of student work was displayed on bright bulletin boards. Posters proclaiming "The world is a rainbow" were hung on the walls. The teacher's desk was piled with papers and books.

"Let's see, where are they," says Mrs. Sommerday as she shuffles through several stacks on her desk. "Uh, here they are. Okay," she addresses the class, "here are the things you ordered." She passes out some rosaries and some silver crucifixes on black cord. She does not appear much older than the students she is teaching.

"Wow, can we still order some more?" a student asks when he sees the silver crosses.

"Gee, well, no, I don't really want to go through that again. Sorry," she answers. I was surprised to see the religious items. I hadn't seen Catholic schools hand out rosaries in years. To me, they were artifacts of an era gone by.

"Look," continued Mrs. Sommerday, speaking loudly to be heard above the class' chatting and shuffling of papers and books, "I just got another lecture about gum chewing—from God," she grimaces. Her tone is sarcastic. The kids buzz about this comment, and Mrs. Sommerday just rolls her eyes and says, "Just don't do it, okay; you know how she gets about it." I assume "God" is Eleanor. There is whispering among the kids about her reaction to gum in school. They don't hassle Mrs. Sommerday about it and seem to bond with her in their perception of Eleanor's role. Some commiserate aloud with their defiant young teacher.

The religion classes she offers are a mixture of covering mandated content material perfunctorily, discussing "issues" assumed to affect teenagers, and just chatting about school, her own personal life, and random interests.

"I don't like the religion books we have," she told me quietly in the hallway the first day I came. Sister Eleanor was nearby. "I do mostly worksheets in groups. I don't really agree with the religion books we have. I don't know, I just don't agree with them. They do better with the sheets."

This emergent teacher had found a way to get around Eleanor's ideas about religion class and reconcile them with her own conceptions of religion for junior high students in the twentieth century. Her curriculum was a curious patchwork of the traditional and a rather loosely defined social-humanistic approach to religion, heavily laced with values. She appeared to have a vague idea of something she would accomplish during each class, filling in the remaining time just conversing with the students. She was sometimes open to the students' ideas about what to do with their time. Her classes stood in stark contrast to the structured, silent lecture/note format of Mrs. Wright.

Some days she just passed out religion quizzes and had the students grade each other's papers and then called them to state their grades aloud as she recorded them. Once, when they also had to figure out a percentage, she called on Alejandro. He just answered, "Messed up." No reprimands from Mrs. Sommerday; she just passed out another quiz to be group-graded. The kids shout out answers all at once; she shouts the correct one to be heard above them and within minutes they are reciting their next grades to her one by one. Alejandro gets 100% on this next quiz, on which there was a lot of room for personal interpretations about asking God for help. I am quite sure that much of the language that gets exchanged during this period is incomprehensible to Alejandro but, as usual, he manages somehow to get by.

The class asks for a reward because so many of them received 100% on the quiz.

"Okay," she says. "I can give you a sticker or I can give you a kiss." They laugh and she passes out candy kisses. Alejandro makes a comment and she laughs and says to him, "Oh, you want a real kiss? Pucker up!" They both laugh and he blushes. What a welcomed respite this period must be for Alejandro, who has most of his other subjects with Mrs. Wright.

As they are eating their candy kisses that morning, the class sees Mrs. Wright rush down the hallway. It is about an hour into the day. They hush and several groan, "Oh, man! She's here." They are clearly disappointed to see her. Alejandro had mentioned that Mrs. Wright had been sick and absent, a rare occurrence for this teacher.

Mrs. Sommerday fills the rest of the hour-long period by reading some cards that describe difficult situations and asking what students would do if faced with such situations. From "Would you date a person who you know has a bad reputation and spreads rumors?" to "Would you tell your grandparents you don't like a gift they gave you?" she ambles through the cards at random and does most of the answering for the students, who shout out short responses that she rephrases and embellishes. It is very moralistic, didactic, and often sexist but done in a very relaxed way. Mrs. Sommerday will even describe something as a "bitch" or talk about being "pissed off," with no realization of the rarity with which parochial elementary school teachers use such relaxed language in a classroom setting.

Over the phone, on one occasion Alejandro used the phrase "pissed off." This surprised me, for he is very aware of my position of *maestra* and accords me the respect he has been taught for that profession. I realized that Alejandro, who hears mainstream English only in school, had no way of realizing the inappropriateness of some of the language this young teacher routinely uses and was adopting it into his own limited English repertoire of sanctioned vocabulary.

Mrs. Sommerday, armed with a book of issue-based questions and scenarios called *What's Right?*, did not shrink from discussing drug problems, sex, drinking, or school behavior. But there was always a clear "right" answer waiting in the wings. When I observed, she elaborated upon the group's short comments and did a lot of the answering herself. I found her thoughts particularly curious one day. She presented a question from one of her supplemental texts that asked if students had ever really acted up in class so much so as to move a teacher to tears. No one offered any comments.

"Well, you'll probably do it someday, maybe in high school with young teachers," she said. "You'll probably do it less or not at all with a man teacher. Why would that be?" she asked. Again, answers were scantily mumbled, and she answered herself. "Well, a female teacher is more sensitive; you'd be more apt to be able to make her cry." For a young woman in her twenties, I found her ideas often conservative, stereotypical, and sexist, although her appearance and language seemed contemporary.

During drug and alcohol awareness week, she valiantly attempts to get her class to discuss these issues with her. "Who has ever had alcohol here?" she asks. The class mumbles, there are a few snickers, about half of the kids raise their hands. Alejandro does not. She tries to get them to talk about parties and drinking, but no one will contribute. Once again, it is her discussion with herself in front of them. "Has anyone ever refused a drink?" Alejandro raises his hand. In her class he attempts to participate. "Why did you refuse it," she asks him.

"I didn't like the taste," he answers softly.

"What did they offer you, beer?" she pursues.

Alejandro says yes.

"Okay, let's talk about hard liquor versus beer," she continues, and begins to chat about various choices in drinks. The class is a little incredulous. There are lots of grins and glances going on. The kids are very tight-lipped. They will not participate much in this conversation. Afterwards, Alejandro mentions to me that he knows the kids have tried liquor. They just weren't talking. Although Mrs. Sommerday may be able to hold such a conversation, clearly the students are not accustomed to such openness about taboo activities.

During the spring, Mrs. Sommerday mentioned that she took her religion class to church on Fridays to do the "Stations of the Cross." Though a dying tradition in many American Catholic communities, Sorrowful Mother still retains it. This Catholic tradition occurs during Lent, which is the liturgical season leading up to the celebration of Easter. It entails recalling and praying at 14 highlighted occurrences as Christ made his way to the hill upon which he was crucified. Every Catholic church will have these 14 scenes displayed in plaster, wood, metal relief, or paint somewhere in the building. I remembered kneeling through dreary Friday "Stations" from my own parochial school experience as a child more than 30 years earlier. I recalled nothing more somber and depressing than Stations of the Cross in dimly lit, stuffy churches with hard wooden kneelers on warm spring Friday afternoons. But Mrs. Sommerday had a way to break out of that 1950s scene—she decided to substitute the traditional visit to the "Stations" with a play.

"Let's act out the Stations of the Cross!" she announced one sunny spring afternoon. "Let's see," it was obvious she was making up this class on the spur of the moment. "Who'll volunteer to be Christ?" she asked. Alejandro raised his hand. "You'll be Christ, Alejandro?" Mrs. Sommerday asks in surprise. "Great!" She glances toward me excitedly. She too had remarked when I first approached her for permission to observe that Alejandro doesn't speak up much in her class.

A rowdy, even bawdy, rendition of the Stations of the Cross ensued. Julie, a loud, heavy set girl with sideburns and a frizzy pony tail, jumps at the chance to be Christ's mother, Mary. John, the class cut-up, volunteers to be one of the weeping women and sobs uncontrollably on cue. All improvise their lines as the class noisily suggests from the sidelines the script for the main players. At one point, Mrs. Sommerday has to get the Station's book out to make sure they are doing things in order. Everyone is totally enjoying this priceless event.

Alejandro is carrying a yardstick as a crucifix, and his classmates give him directions, half in English, half in Spanish, concerning where to walk and what to say. In his faltering English he manages to deliver appropriate lines.

A female student teases and calls out, "Are you going to take off your clothes too?" One of the first stations recounts the striping of Christ's cloak from his body.

"No!" cries Alejandro and they all laugh.

"Trip him, he's supposed to fall for the first time," another boy shouts. Alejandro is now kneeling on the classroom floor. Julie, who is playing Mary, comes to him and says, "I love you, why don't you do something about all of this?" The class roars. But she is actually very loosely interpreting a key occurrence in the "Stations" when Christ's mother calls upon Him to use his Godly powers to rectify a situation.

Alejandro falters for an answer, and Mrs. Sommerday and the class give him suggestions. He finally says, "I have to die for the people who have sins."

They progress through scenes where a follower helps Alejandro with the yardstick cross and the woman named Veronica wipes his face. When he reaches the weeping women, John steals the scene as he cries hysterically, and Alejandro ad libs hesitantly, saying, "Don't cry. I'm gonna save your sins." We all laugh so hard that tears are rolling down our faces as John truly gets wrapped up in his role.

All the time Mrs. Sommerday is keeping things honest and reciting from her book what should occur next. Alejandro reaches the top of the mountain.

"What's the top of the mountain called?" asks the teacher. No one knows. "Is it Mt. Rushmore? Calvary?" They recognize her prompt and reply in unison, "Calvary!"

"What do they do now?" she asks.

"Strip him!" squeal the girls. "Wow!" Mrs. Sommerday shakes her head, "You guys are bad," she laughs.

Alejandro is now standing on a chair, arms outstretched. Julie approaches and says, "He's supposed to say 'God bless these people; they don't know what they're doing.'" To my surprise, Alejandro is able to remember and repeat her cue, then pretends to die and glances toward me. Julie, playing Mary, screams, "Oh no, my son!" and the melodrama winds down. They pretend to entomb Christ and the bell for the end of class rings.

"You all have an A for today," calls the teacher as they rush out to their next class, still buzzing about the performance.

Mrs. Sommerday congratulates the actors and comes over to me. "I was so surprised that Alejandro volunteered to be Christ. I thought he did it because you were here!"

I agreed and told her how much I enjoyed the whole event and how I appreciated Alejandro's attempt to participate. I wondered how Eleanor would have reacted to the play. Though a raucous, bold interpretation, there was a genuine concern on the part of the class to re-enact the Stations accurately, to include key events and statements they recalled. I thought to myself, Alejandro will remember that class and the "Stations" better than he ever would have just by reciting them traditionally. Sacrilege or success?—it was all in the eyes of the beholder.

As I followed Alejandro to his next class, remedial reading, I congratulated him on his efforts. He was so delighted with his performance that he could barely explain it to his reading teacher. "Sorry I'm late, Ms. Gonzales," he said excitedly. "I had to be Christ in my last class."

Doubting Hearts

Alejandro? He's a great kid; he'll do anything you ask.

—Mrs. Lago

During May I found teachers at Sorrowful Mother increasingly reluctant to have me visit their classrooms. Ms. Gonzales reported that Alejandro was missing his remedial reading classes frequently because of tests and activities in his homeroom. She felt frustrated but resigned to the situation. She was leaving Sorrowful Mother at the end of the year and just wanted to finish up without problems from Eleanor or anyone else at the school. "That whole group of junior high teachers aren't friendly to me. They just seem to keep in their own little clique. I don't like how they are with the students, not only with Alejandro. I don't get involved," she had confided to me. Mrs. Wright seemed to be giving more and more study time in class (at least when I wanted to visit); Mr. James was giving math tests; and Mrs. Sommerday, usually my only easy entry point, told me that Sister Eleanor was hassling her about my visits.

"But she gave me permission earlier in the year," I said. "I made sure to clear everything with her before I planned my whole study."

"Well, I don't know what's going on with her but she asked me why you're here so much. She said she didn't like it. Would you just remind her about what she said to you?" She sounded annoyed. I'm sure she didn't need any pressure from the principal she referred to as "God."

"I'll speak to her today," I told Mrs. Sommerday. "I've appreciated your help and I don't want to cause any problems for you."

I did speak to Sister Eleanor and she said I had asked her a long time ago and I should have reminded her again. I explained once more that my study was covering the whole academic year. I also informed her that I always asked the individual teachers about specific visits repeatedly but that I didn't think I needed to ask her repeatedly. It was "okay" she ended up saying, but it was clear that she didn't give me her blessing in my work. She never told me that I couldn't visit or indicated that it actually bothered her, as she did to Mrs. Sommerday, and I continued to try to observe Alejandro in his school setting right up until his graduation. I felt that I had lost important observation time due to an illness in April and I wanted to make use of all the school time that was left in the year.

I had found that the majority of Alejandro's classes were traditional teacher-controlled lecture/note taking or lecture/worksheet-workbook-written exercise classes, a format to which Alejandro responded very passively. Although I was getting a fairly good picture of teacher expectations and styles, I wanted to know more about Alejandro's interactions with and impression on teachers before the school year ended for him. So, in May, when I realized that, despite clarifying my intentions with Eleanor, it had become even more difficult to observe actual classes, I decided to formally interview each of Alejandro's main teachers. The teachers were winding down for the year and just did not want "interlopers" in their rooms.

I wondered what the teachers really felt about this student, Alejandro Juarez, Jr., who sat before them every day and so obviously struggled to complete the assignments they gave him. He enjoyed the antics of his peers immensely and could easily appear not to take school seriously. Yet at home, he truly put effort into the frustrating assignments he received. I saw little individual interaction between Alejandro and his teachers in the junior high classes. When Alejandro attempted to engage his teachers in conversation he typically tried to make jokes, which they could not always follow due to his faltering English.

What did these teachers really know about Alejandro's world? I decided to prepare six specific questions I wanted to ask them after they had had Alejandro as a student all year.

- What did they see as his strengths in school?
- His weaknesses?
- What did they think of his English language proficiency?
- How did he relate to peers in their estimations?
- What did they think his major obstacles in high school would be?
- In general, was there anything else they'd like to say about Alejandro?

I wanted to give them a chance to share anything that they wanted me to know about him.

Again I was confronted with reluctance, but one by one I set up appointments with Alejandro's teachers. Most preferred to meet briefly during school time and leave their classes with seatwork, although I offered to meet before or after school hours, during free periods, whenever it was most convenient for them.

"I can give you 10 minutes," Mrs. Wright told me. "It's best for me if you come during class time." Mr. James voiced the same preference. "I can meet during class if I know which day you're coming," he informed me.

Mrs. Lago, the computer teacher, and Mr. James, math, answered my inquiries thoughtfully, in an unharried manner. Ms. Gonzales, of special interest to me as Alejandro's remedial reading teacher, met with me off-campus, during the summer, because she had been so busy with plans for her wedding and had arranged to end teaching earlier than regular classes ended. She also put time and thought into her interview responses. Mrs. Sommerday and Mrs. Wright were polite but rushed through their answers and responded very briefly to my openended, final question.

Only one teacher, Mrs. Sommerday, agreed to meet after school. I am sure she had forgotten our appointment because on the day we scheduled to meet together, I entered the junior high hallway shortly before dismissal and saw that she had her class lined up in the corridor. At the first sound of the final bell she locked her classroom door and turned to leave, book bag in hand. When she saw me her face dropped and she said, "Uh, I was thinking, why don't we meet downstairs?"

"That'll be fine," I answered. "Thanks so much for giving me this time." I tried in vain to engage in conversation with her but she had changed perceptibly since our early meetings before Sister Eleanor voiced disapproval of my access to religion classes. Mrs. Sommerday seemed more guarded and less friendly.

With the exception of Ms. Gonzales, who met with Alejandro alone or with one additional student, all of the teachers felt that Alejandro was well liked by his peers despite their awareness of his severe academic problems. In addition, the teachers expressed concerns that he could become distracted from schoolwork by peers. Mrs. Sommerday and Mr. James expressed that type of concern in even stronger terms, feeling that Alejandro might "succumb" to peer pressure or "do anything" to be accepted.

It appeared to me that only Mrs. Lago and Ms. Gonzales had any accurate idea of what Alejandro's home situation was like. Ms. Gonzales's awareness was due to the Juarezes' participation in the summer ESL program in which she taught Alejandro's youngest sister and made a home visit in connection with writing a mini-ethnography based on Lupita's home context. Mrs. Lago was the only other classroom

teacher who had spoken at length with Mrs. Juarez. Although she did
not share Mrs. Juarez's ethnic background, they did share the same
native language, so communication was not hindered between them.
I was impressed with her awareness of Alejandro's home situation,
namely, caring and concerned parents unable to offer academic help
due to their own limited educational backgrounds. I was impressed also
by her understanding of Alejandro's good intentions and caring nature, for I had not noticed a particular recognition of that in class. In
fact, the day I came to interview Mrs. Lago, Alejandro was helping her
clean the computer lab and was mopping her room as a punishment
for forgetfulness. Due to this particular punishment, Alejandro had
missed the cake I had brought to his class that day in appreciation for
the students opening their educational lives to me. I had received Mrs.
Wright's permission for the treat and Alejandro's input as to what to
bring and was disappointed that Mrs. Wright seemed not to even notice that Alejandro was not able to participate in the little celebration.

As Mrs. Lago and I talked, Alejandro was finally permitted to go
back to his homeroom. He returned in minutes with slices of chocolate cake and pop for Mrs. Lago, her aide, and me. Mrs. Lago had just
finished saying to me, "He's a great kid. He'll do anything you ask . . .
he doesn't give any problems."

"See what I mean," she smiled as Alejandro walked in excitedly
with the food.

Mrs. Lago felt that Alejandro's strengths were his respect for teachers and his peers, and she spoke of the growth she had seen in him over
the past 4 years.

"When I first met him, he couldn't read a single story off the computer. He can now; he's still at the low level, but he can read now."

Mrs. Lago worried though, that Alejandro does not "believe in
himself," does not believe he can achieve in school and will not give
himself "a second chance." "He says, 'It's hard, I just can't do it,'"
reported Mrs. Lago.

"Even if I beg him to try," said Mrs. Lago, "Alejandro gives up."
She pointed to what she saw as a lack of concentration on Alejandro's
part, increased by his enjoyment of his peers and a lack of self-confidence.

"But you know, he gets along with his classmates despite all of his
problems. I've seen a lot of kids like him who don't." I agreed with
Mrs. Lago's observation. Somehow, Alejandro manages to plod along,
to cover up the extent of his pervasive academic problems, and, to his
delight, to be an unridiculed part of the group.

Mr. James felt that in his math class Alejandro gave "an honest
effort to understand" but that he was "easily distracted" and needed

to "review constantly or he'll forget what he just did." He described
Alejandro's English language proficiency as "adequate for math." When
I probed as to the reasons he was going to fail math, Mr. James said it
was a "combination of things" but that basically, "he doesn't remember. In eighth grade there are so many things in math they need to
know. He has to remember everything. He has nothing memorized."

Mr. James made an interesting comment at the end of his interview regarding Alejandro's group. "He gets along with everybody; he
has a lot of friends. From what I see, no one seems to put down the
fact that he goes for extra help. . . . Of course, as a whole, that group
isn't one of the highest eighth grades we've ever had. That class is
negative and lazy. You know, I think if he had been with a different
class, a better group, he would have been a lot better off." He spoke of
his belief that Alejandro's class really added to his problems because
they clowned around so much, were sarcastic, and just weren't strong
or motivated students.

"If he were with a better class, like the seventh graders, I think he
would have been encouraged to try harder. They would have been a
better influence on him."

I had similar feelings about Alejandro's class, although I didn't
blame them for what I saw frequently as a flat response to school. For
all of them, I felt, school was clearly a place to perform for teachers, to
run the obstacle course, and they were going to do that with as little
effort as possible. Their education was not exciting, not particularly
meaningful to them. From what I observed, it seemed that they were
not often encouraged to think or act creatively. They were recipients
of a skills-based philosophy of education.

Mrs. Wright, in contrast to Mrs. Lago, described Alejandro as "self-
assured" but echoed Mrs. Lago's feeling that Alejandro "thinks he's
going to fail before he does it . . . he just doesn't try very hard." Her
familiar complaint about Alejandro not trying hard enough surfaced
repeatedly during her interview.

Like the other teachers, she noted that Alejandro related well with
his peers. "I think he's very aware of his academic problems," she commented. I think the other kids are aware of his problems and seem to
wait for his answers; they don't really make fun of him." Throughout
the interview she stood, as I sat writing, even when I offered her a chair.
I felt very small and somewhat inhibited as she hurriedly went through
this activity with me.

When asked about Alejandro's parents, Mrs. Wright answered, "I
think they hold him back [pause] well, unwillingly." In many of her
responses she made a statement quickly and then qualified it further.

"I think they want the best for him but they're unwilling [pause] or not able to help. I'm sure everything is in Spanish." I felt distinctly that Mrs. Wright tempered her answers because I was there and tacked on afterthoughts to soften the blow of her initial answers.

I was surprised that in response to my question regarding Alejandro's English language proficiency, Mrs. Wright described it as below level but very good "for someone who didn't start using English, what, till about 2 years ago?" Actually it was about 5 years earlier that Alejandro had returned to Sorrowful Mother. Mrs. Wright continued, "I couldn't tell you what grade level I'd assume him to be. In some things he'd be near level and other things are further from him." She seemed to minimize the extent of Alejandro's language and learning problems, although she knew he had failed all his classes all year.

Most teachers expressed some compassion and concern for Alejandro in the open-ended, final question, Is there anything else you'd like to tell me about Alejandro? But Mrs. Wright, lowering her voice, said, "I think you should know that Alejandro has a definite tendency to cheat. He cheated on a science test last week. I know he's a cheater. I'm sure he's getting help from someone, from whatever source [pause]. I think that it stems from his insecurity with work." She seemed to attach the last statement to her indictment as a perfunctory afterthought as she looked at my face, a rare occurrence in my conversation with this teacher. Her tone betrayed a sense of dutifully telling me something dark and ominous that I needed to know. Her thick accent hung in the air, "I know he's a chea-tah."

I thanked Mrs. Wright for her time and made no comment about the cheating and her condemnation of Alejandro, which was evident in her lowered tone as she alerted me to her suppositions.

Unlike Mrs. Wright, I did avail myself of Alejandro's evaluation and had knowledge of his grade levels in various content areas. He had been tested at the college a few years earlier due to his learning problems yet no one at Sorrowful Mother seemed to accept the findings in the written report describing his learning disabilities, which had been given to the principal.

In his most recent evaluation (summer 1993), Alejandro had managed to improve his decoding abilities to place him around the fifteenth percentile on standardized reading tests (Stanford Diagnostic Reading Test, Woodcock Reading Mastery Test—Revised). Yet his comprehension was only between the first and third percentile on several standardized reading tests. His spelling was below the first percentile, and his knowledge of math concepts at the first percentile.

Underlying skills in expressive vocabulary were at the third percentile, comprehension of grammatical structures in the range of less than the first percentile to about the second percentile, and comprehension of vocabulary at the first percentile (Peabody Picture Vocabulary Test—Revised). His actual reading grade score placed him at a beginning third-grade level.

Interestingly, Alejandro recently was assessed as English dominant based on a standardized language dominance test given during the summer ESL program. His English proficiency was rated slightly higher than his Spanish proficiency. But in this test, as is the case for many current language dominance instruments, only conversational skills are assessed rather than the more complex language needed for academic work. Nestled in the security of his home, Spanish was his language of choice even if some words escaped him. I had seen him repeatedly, throughout the year, switch into Spanish at moments he felt most at ease with family and friends. No language dominance test I knew could measure the effect of context.

Although the standardized tests used to arrive at these percentiles and grade levels are historically biased against minority students and even more inadequate for linguistically diverse students, they give a glimpse, I feel, of what Alejandro is up against. His diagnostician was a well-balanced bilingual L.D. specialist, which is a luxury many second language children are not afforded in the assessment process. Frequently, untrained bilingual teacher aides or parent volunteers end up translating and administering tests, if any attempt to be language sensitive is undertaken in districts. At other times, examiners with different accents and pronunciation patterns emanating from European Spanish versus Central, Caribbean, or South American Spanish administer the few Spanish language tests available. The results, for example, might be that a Puerto Rican diagnostician administers a crucial test in a Puerto Rican accent, using some key vocabulary typical to that island, to a Mexican child. A roughly analogous situation might be a British examiner using British pronunciation and vocabulary to test an American English-speaking child. The problems in bilingual assessment are multifaceted.

Yet, Alejandro scored strongly within the average range, at the forty-seventh and ninety-second percentiles, on nonverbal mental ability tests. Luz, his diagnostician, who had tested him in fifth grade as well, and I were delighted to see those scores. It gave some credence to our suspicion that mainstream language depressed other scores significantly.

In addition to language, Luz and I remained convinced that a memory problem and visual perception weakness hindered Alejandro's performance. Luz noted that she thought his math score would not have been so low if he could just have remembered the operational signs. He still confused the plus sign with the sign for multiplication. In my work with Alejandro over several years I have noticed such confusion, as well as reversals of *b* and *d*, inversions of *n* and *u*, in addition to confusion between English and Spanish vowels. I have even observed that he reads more accurately when his book is turned sideways, rather than placed in front of him. Much of what I observed are hallmarks of dyslexia, a severe reading problem that calls for intensive remediation.

In short, I felt like commending Alejandro for what Wright called "cheating." I could not help but admire Alejandro's attempts to somehow succeed, even minimally, in school, faced as he was with teachers who ignored his severe academic and processing problems, despite concrete indications of them in his formal assessment. He sought to collaborate on homework assignments, on long-range projects, and on classwork. In fact, collaborative grouping or a buddy system was suggested in his educational evaluation on file at Sorrowful Mother. In frustration and anxiety, I am sure, he sought help in tests as well.

The interviews I conducted showed that his teachers, with the exception of remedial reading, chose to explain his academic problems as lack of sufficient effort. Even Mr. James, although aware of memory problems affecting math, pointed to peers and low self-expectations as underlying problems in his math achievement. None, not even the remedial reading teacher, voiced major concern about his lack of English proficiency. In a school of 99–100% Latino enrollment, it obviously becomes easy to overlook second language difficulties as nonstandard English becomes the norm. Most described Alejandro's English as "adequate," "below level but . . . very good," "improved," "fine." Some qualified their answers a bit, speaking of his good conversational abilities but persistent reading problems. I found their perceptions in this area interesting, for I would not call even his conversational English "fine." Alejandro often searches for words to express himself when engaged in extended discourse and routinely mismatches verbs and nouns, floundering for vocabulary.

I spoke at length to his remedial reading teacher since I felt that complete literacy is such a major issue in the life of Alejandro and his family. Had she found any methodology that seemed to help him, I asked her, did she see any improvement? Her responses were disappointing to me. Yes, she had found that mapping activities (in which a teacher discusses and diagrams key points in a story before or after reading it) seemed to help him but she did not use them consistently. Yes, she found that motivating materials really aided his comprehension, particularly if dealing with sports or simplified current events of interest. Yes, she had seen some improvement in reading and discussion of reading, but in writing and spelling, "no way, there was no significant improvement." What she spoke of frequently was her frustration in scheduling, meeting with him only 50 minutes a week and losing even that once spring came around.

"What would you have done, if you had had more time with him?" I asked.

"I would really have gone through the material and talked about the reading and helped him to make connections, make him really think about things" she responded. I knew that she was working with incredibly limited time and resources and that Alejandro had deep-rooted and complex problems, far too complex to treat quickly in an interview. When I observed in her classes, I saw that she put effort into finding interesting reading material at a comprehensible level. Due to her time constraints, her selections were short, frequently from magazines geared for middle-grade students. Her help revolved primarily around pointing out errors and encouraging her students to "try again" or "think about it." I felt she was strongest when she used her own first language, which matched her students', to clarify vocabulary.

"Sometimes I wonder if it's too late for Alejandro," I confided in her. She worried about that, too. An English as a second language speaker herself, she struggled to communicate her feelings. She confided that she avoided using phonics-related methodologies in her classes for that was not a strength in her own teaching. I knew that Alejandro had been drilled in English phonics for years and I doubted that more phonics would have helped him, anyway. I wondered if it wouldn't have been better to have Ms. Gonzales work with Alejandro and other students like him in Spanish, which was her strength, instead of English. I knew that a strong basis in the native language could only help in the second idiom, particularly for students like Alejandro, who needed something as basic as learning how to discuss narrative material and express reactions to it in extended discourse.

Occasionally, Ms. Gonzales explained to Alejandro in Spanish and thought to employ Spanish to help his comprehension. In a reading class where he struggled to decode the word "solar," Ms. Gonzales said, "*Sol, sol, el sol*" to him, stressing the Spanish word meaning sun to help him in pronunciation and comprehension of the word used to describe a car of the future run on solar energy. "Ohhh," Alejandro smiled. Ms. Gonzales was able to offer the invaluable skill of biliteracy as an aid to Alejandro, although for only 50 minutes, once a week.

I noticed, both in his remedial reading class and in reading with me, that Alejandro often second guessed his decoding. In an attempt to self-correct, he sometimes actually changed a correctly read word to an error. For example, he read "Zoom, zoom" correctly in the article on cars of the future, then attempted a self-correction and read, "Zum, zum." Self-monitoring is often a more difficult task for second language readers. They do not have the sense of something "sounding right" for they do not hear the language they are reading as they grow up at home.

I had seen the effects myself of the strongly skills- and phonics-based reading program at Sorrowful Mother. The ESL students struggled with a request for anything beyond one- or two-word, pat, and factual responses to literature. Filling in blanks was a consistent form of written language they seemed to encounter in school. Reading and writing at Sorrowful Mother were conceived of primarily as a "cluster of isolable skills" (Edelsky, 1986). Teachers involved with the ESL program over the years had sometimes described their skills-based programs and occasionally sent reading worksheets to be completed in ESL classes.

Ms. Gonzales concluded our interview by saying to me, "It's too many things for Alejandro, it's not just reading. Even if you have the heart to do it, you know, the heart to try, you can't put everything together for him. You know, it's different from working with a first grader with severe problems; we're talking about an eighth, ninth grader now."

That was the final statement of her interview, the last of all the teacher interviews to be completed. Her words hung ominously in my memory. I hoped she was wrong; I hoped that "heart" could help.

In the Belly of the Beast

Chicago lags far behind the growing national effort to find ways to educate the impoverished children of big cities.
—*Forging New Schools*, J. L. Griffin

Crown Metropolitan High School is one of the largest in the Chicago public school system. It houses more than 3,000 culturally and linguistically diverse students divided fairly equally among three major groups: African-Americans, Latinos (mostly Mexican, some Central American and Caribbean), and Caucasians (predominantly of Eastern European descent and some of Irish background). The largest bilingual classes in the school service more than 300 non-English-speaking Polish students, about 30 non-English, Spanish speakers, and a smattering of Chinese and Arabic native language speakers. Although there are many other second language speakers in the school who could use assistance in academic English, they are considered proficient enough to be mainstreamed in regular classes and are not classified as monolingual speakers of a non-English language. Crown is situated in an area experiencing a boom in Polish immigration and must accept neighborhood students despite its magnet school status. For that reason, it has a large Polish bilingual program.

According to school personnel, Crown students segregate voluntarily along ethnic lines, and the school is considered one of the best and safest public high schools in Chicago. The staff at Crown is security-conscious, and any problems, I was told by a staff member, are usually due to oversights or mistakes by supervisors. It is such a large building that every now and then something just slides by; yet, it is not considered a dangerous building within the system. However, serious problems arise outside of the school building, in the immediate school neighborhood. Last year, two Crown students were killed in gang-related shootings very close to the campus.

In many ways Crown epitomizes everything I feared for Alejandro in an urban high school—a huge sprawling building, large numbers, watered down curriculum, impersonalism, gangs, and drugs. In many ways, I felt that placing him there is tantamount to having him swallowed by Jonah's whale, putting him squarely into the belly of the beast.

But Alma, with her ability to stoically accept the cold, hard facts of reality, actively pursued Crown as the high school she chose for her son. She had asked about Catholic secondary school tuition earlier in the year and told me there was just no feasible way they could ever finance such a cost, which ranged from $3,000 to $5,000 a year. Sister Faith had told me that financial aid was usually limited by the Chicago Archdiocese to $500 a year because so many families applied for help. I knew that the Juarez family needed more help with tuition than that figure would supply. In addition, the few Catholic high schools that offered any special educational assistance or vocational programs were far from Alejandro's house and would necessitate hours of travel each day by bus or train even if he was accepted into them with financial aid.

At least Crown offered a technical program about which Alma had heard good things, and we thought such a program would be practical for Alejandro given his severe academic problems. Although I admit it is hard for me to be practical and accept the disappointing reality of educational alternatives for urban, limited-English-proficient students, I realized that an affordable, suitable private high school for Alejandro was an impossible dream on my part. I also grappled with the idea of a vocational program and the fear of limiting Alejandro's possibilities in life. I am a great fan of Freire and his championing of third world voice in pedagogy, and my ideals were crashing headfirst into the brick wall Chicago's educational opportunities for low income, low achieving, second language, minority students presented. How many times had I cautioned my ESL teachers in my courses at the college not to limit adult second language learners to workplace ESL, where students are trained only in vocabulary and idioms peculiar to low level, low paying, nonprofessional jobs like restaurant help? Was I facilitating such a "training" situation for Alejandro? How far could he progress if someone offered him consistent, high quality, thoughtful, and meaningful educational help? Did he have any hope of a college education? These questions filled my mind and troubled my heart. Yet, perhaps one of the many things I had learned from Alma was that there are times when the ideal is so far from the possible that you must resign yourself to what is plausible though lesser.

Our next obstacle was to convince the professionals at Crown to give Alejandro, whose eighth-grade report card was so dismal, a chance to attend their school. Because it was categorized as a "magnet" school, Crown could draw students like Alejandro who were not from the immediate neighborhood. Although I seriously questioned the notion of magnet schools, which can lure the brightest students out of neighborhood schools with the perks of extra equipment and programs, I found myself grateful that there was a feasible alternative to Melton High School for Alejandro. Melton, just two blocks from his home, had a bad reputation for poor scholarship and gang violence. The Juarezes had seen problems occurring firsthand as they rode past the building themselves. And Alma, always able to access neighborhood-based information, had heard frightening things about the school. In addition, I had a friend, Sara Puente, who worked at Crown as a guidance counselor. Sara had worked for the Chicago Board for years and knew the ins and outs of the public school's thick bureaucracy. She described their program to me and suggested the process I should follow to try to get Alejandro considered as a student there. Sara was frank about Crown's problems in a totally professional way, painting an honest picture of what the school could offer without covering up the dangers I asked about. She never directly told me not to advise the Juarezes to seek enrollment at Crown, but she did suggest considering a smaller and safer environment for Alejandro. However, at the other public school to which she alluded, I was told that they did not offer a good program for students with learning problems and they preferred not to consider admitting Alejandro. Crown, at least, would listen to Alejandro's case, and Sara Puente would be there to assist him.

At Sara's suggestion, I wrote a long letter to Crown's principal explaining Alejandro's situation, namely, his lack of consistent special help in parochial school, his rejection from his own overcrowded neighborhood public school, and his diagnostic evaluation substantiating his learning problems. To my surprise, the principal of the school accepted him into their technical program based on my letter. There Alejandro could pursue courses in woodworking, photography, auto mechanics, electrician training, or business and computers in addition to completing the requirements for a bona fide high school diploma. Alma was very pleased with the news but decided not to tell Alejandro right away because Mrs. Wright had just delivered another "he-needs-to-try-harder" lecture to her. She feared that if he knew he had a place secured at Crown, her son would "blow off" the end of eighth grade and jeopardize the possibility of graduating.

Shortly after these arrangements I became ill and was hospitalized. I physically couldn't handle finalizing the paper work and red tape still to be completed to officially register Alejandro at Crown, and the

Juarezes couldn't read enough to complete the forms alone. Sara took over and contacted Alma during that period, asking her to deliver Alejandro's report card to the director of Crown's technical program, Mr. Waters. When Mr. Waters saw his grades, the offer for Alejandro to attend Crown was rescinded. Sara Puente called me at home to discuss the problem.

"I hate to be the bearer of bad news when you're supposed to be recovering, but his grades were just so bad that Mr. Waters reconsidered things and he has the last say on the technical program. You know, I heard that Melton High School has a new principal; maybe things will get better there. I think you're really going to have to convince Alma to consider that for Alejandro." Sara knew how apprehensive Alma was of Melton and high school in general. "I feel so bad. That poor mother just looked so scared when she came to Crown. It's like it's her and this little family up against the whole world," commented Sara.

I felt terrible. I couldn't help but think that if I could have followed up on things myself, none of this would have happened. I called Melton High School and started to find out what programs they had in ESL or learning disabilities. Their answers were vague; they spoke of having to accept Alejandro at Shepherd School long enough to be tested. The paper work sounded incredible and I knew that no one at the Juarez home could manage it. I talked to Sara Puente again and asked her if there wasn't anything we could try at Crown to get them to reconsider Alejandro. I explained to her what I had observed about the teachers at Sorrowful Mother—the absence of any remedial plan or ability to individualize for a student with such severe learning problems. She suggested another letter, this time to Mr. Waters, explaining in particular Alejandro's eighth-grade situation. I wrote the most heartfelt letter I could and basically begged Mr. Waters to give a "good boy," who has had a lot of bad breaks educationally, a chance. I promised help from the college's tutoring programs and my own help. Mr. Waters agreed to meet with Alma, Alejandro, and me—we had our second chance.

I picked up Alejandro and his mom early on the morning of our appointment at Crown.

"What time do you think we'll be done?" asked Alejandro. "My class is gonna wait for me to go to a White Sox game. Sister Eleanor promised they'd wait for me."

"I don't think we'll be long and I'll drive you right over to school," I said. I knew field trips were a cherished event for Alejandro, one of the few opportunities he had to be with his peers outside of school. I was impressed that Eleanor had promised they'd wait for him due to a meeting at a *public* high school. She never ceased to confuse and amaze me.

We drove toward Crown, which is only a few miles from Alejandro's home, and waited for a red light in front of the school, heading for a parking lot on the far west side of the large building. Alejandro noticed the gang graffiti sprayed over the low walls that encircle trees in front of the school.

"Do you know about the O t B's? You can graduate from being an O t B to a King. Kings are the best, I think." I looked toward Alma to see if she was comprehending any of this conversation. Alejandro rarely ever spoke in Spanish to me, only if he couldn't remember a particular word as he related an event. She gazed straight ahead. I doubted she comprehended any of what her son had said in English.

Alejandro continued, "See those lines over there," he traced the design in the air again. "Those are the 2–6's. That's their sign, lines just like that. I don't care so much for the 2–6's. They don't have anything like the Kings," he grinned.

"Where did you learn about all of this?" I asked in amazement. I was stunned not only because Alejandro was often so innocent about things going on around him but also because he found it so extremely difficult to correctly name letters in English or Spanish. Numbers were hard for him as well. This problem was so pronounced for him that we had developed a system during tutoring so that when he asked how to spell a word for homework, I wrote the letters he needed on scrap paper for him. Otherwise he could not transcribe them from verbal cues. Yet he could relate, correctly, all the gang symbols and letters he saw on a short gray wall at least 50 feet away on an overcast morning.

"The boys in my class tell me. But they tell me to don't be stupid and don't join gangs. Only one kid tries to get kids to join gangs. He's in seventh grade but he should be in high school," Alejandro explained.

I couldn't resist adding my own admonitions against gangs, and Alejandro, who loved to tease, laughed and told me not to worry. "I would never do it, Chris. I just like knowing about the signs and stuff."

When we entered the building, Alma found a public phone and wanted to call her younger children to be sure they had gotten ready for school. She dialed her number then quickly hung up, looking afraid.

"Me hablaron en inglés!" ["They're saying something to me in English!"] she said to Alejandro. "Do it for me; you try." She turned to me and said, "I don't know what happened. Maybe I put in the wrong amount of money."

I said, yes, that some phones were a quarter and others cost more. Alejandro got through to his house momentarily and Alma, taking the phone's receiver cautiously, spoke briefly to her other children, reminding them to lock the doors.

Her reaction at the pay phone surprised me. She completely panicked when the recorded message came in English. Second language presents such a barrier to Alma. Her world is so constricted by her inability to handle English. Even a simple call on a public phone to her children can become a difficult hurdle for her to overcome. Without basic English abilities, I thought, it must in fact seem that she and her family *are* up against the whole world, as Sara Puente had commented. A children's novel I once read, *Island of the Blue Dolphins* (O'Dell, 1960), related the story of a native woman who survived alone for almost 20 years on a Pacific island until missionaries discovered her. The island was in actuality only 75 miles off the coast of California, and by the time she was found, her own indigenous culture and language had died away and disappeared. Somehow the Juarezes brought that story to my mind. Their struggle with English seemed as insurmountable and effective in cutting them off from full participation in society as did the 75 miles of water between the lost woman on the island and human contact on the California coast.

The meeting with Mr. Waters was brief. He introduced himself and shook hands; Sara and I translated his main points for Alma. As soon as we sat in his office he looked directly at Alejandro and said, "I don't like this report card of yours at all. I'm especially concerned about these low effort marks. I can understand about problems you have with schoolwork but I can't understand low effort grades. If you come here, you've got to work hard, if not, you're out." There it was; direct and to the point. Alejandro cast his eyes downward; Alma looked frightened.

I didn't know about the low effort grades. I was surprised and angry. It was Mrs. Wright's subjects that had the low effort marks. I thought that at least Mrs. Wright would have acknowledged Alejandro's attempts.

"You know, Mr. Waters," I said, "I've worked all year with Alejandro on his homework assignments. So has his godmother and cousin. His parents tell me that he stays up late struggling to do his homework. I really don't think those effort grades are a fair representation of him. I don't think his teacher really accepts his learning problems and doesn't understand how hard he really tries."

"Well, that makes me feel a little better about things," said Mr. Waters. "But I'm telling you, young man," he looked at Alejandro, "I expect you to work hard in our program. We'll do everything we can to get you through it, but you've got to do your part." Alejandro mumbled an affirmative answer, eyes still cast down. Alma didn't say a word.

Mr. Waters talked about the program he directed, the new computers they had, the high caliber of what they offered despite the bad press coverage they had received recently due to after-school gang violence. "The press never talks about anything that goes right. They just jump on a story about the bad Chicago public schools and they can always find some parent to agree with it. It really gets me mad because we have an excellent program."

He and Sara then discussed which courses Alejandro would take his freshman year. Unfortunately, his first choice for the technical program, auto mechanics, was filled. So was carpentry, his second choice. But there was room for him in the business strand or photography. Alma and Alejandro chose the business course. They both seemed bewildered by this new step in Alejandro's educational journey. I hoped business would work out for him. He had told me that he loved to type and Mrs. Lago said he enjoyed computers. Crown's business program concentrated heavily on computers.

Alejandro would take what was called ESL II English, a course tailored to second language speakers at an intermediate level; ethnic history, a social studies course concentrating on minorities; low level algebra; and introduction to business/computers. He would receive one period a day for L.D. class, which consisted of a teacher aide who would help him with his homework. Sara stressed that Alejandro had to ask specifically for help in his assignments or the tutor would not work with him that day.

"They really want the students to be responsible for their own progress," she explained.

It surprised me that they called homework help their severe L.D. program. I think Crown, like many other high schools, follows a compensatory rather than remedial philosophy concerning students with learning problems. Rather than trying to strengthen and develop learning abilities, they water down programs. They simplify the curriculum in response to learners' difficulties; there is no conception of pursuing new paradigms in education, altering methodologies, individualizing teaching, or building up weaknesses by using strengths. Remedial efforts, by and large, are left to elementary school L.D. programs.

Given the severe challenges Alejandro faced, and his past school experiences, I hoped that the watered down curriculum would give him a better chance to succeed academically than he had before. My convictions continue to crash into the walls of reality, but I cannot relinquish hope for improvement, particularly in complete literacy, for this young man. Although his teachers' doubts ring in my ears, I will not give up my "heart" to try to offer something more than threats and lowered expectations for a student who has had to cross so many borders in his young life. Daily as he crosses physically through neighborhoods where his mere looks make him suspect of crimes, daily when he emerges from a home steeped in Spanish language and Mexican culture, daily as he enters schools where his background of experiences mismatches teachers' expectations, he confronts multiple barriers to his hopes and dreams.

In the library in my town, there is a poster at the front door that says, "That all may read . . ." and advertises special services for the deaf and blind through the suburban library system. I think of Alejandro when I see that poster and wonder what special services can be offered to an individual whose challenge is not so apparent as blindness or deafness, but that, in this affluent nation of ours, can cut off children from participation in the benefits of literacy as effectively as sensory deprivation does. As I draw my study of this student to an end, I find that I am left with more questions than I began with, of greater magnitude and of more urgency than I had imagined. What can we do educationally for the Alejandros of this world? What can I do for Alejandro Juarez?

Stormy Weather

Yo soy un good boy.

—Alejandro Juarez, Jr.

Notes from school were a challenge to the Juarez family, six of whose seven members experienced great difficulties in reading. Only Ricardo, the youngest son, a first grader, seemed able to handle English literacy with ease. The Juarez family car was bedecked in bright yellow bumper stickers proclaiming that they have an honor student at their neighborhood school. And Ricardo proudly pointed out, "It's me!" I believe that one day soon Ricardo will become the primary translator and reader for family business. Until then, the Juarezes make what sense they are able to of the communications sent home from school. Whether in English or Spanish, they present challenges.

Alma called one Sunday night close to Alejandro's graduation and invited me to graduation and a dinner sponsored by the school. Her understanding of the note sent home about the event was that she could purchase tickets for friends and family.

"We want you to come, Christina, as our guest," she said. "I know other families who have brought guests." She would double-check the exact date and time, which she had forgotten, but if I was interested, she would go ahead and order an extra ticket.

I accepted her invitation gladly but told her that I would ask Sister Eleanor if she would give me a ticket since I worked in the school. Ten dollar tickets are no small cost for families who struggle to meet the everyday expenses of life. I asked Sister Eleanor that week if I could purchase a ticket for graduation.

"What do you mean?" she scowled.

"I heard there were tickets for a graduation dinner next week and I was hoping to attend," I responded.

"Well, graduation is in the church and you don't need a ticket. There's a graduation Mass on Saturday at 9:00."

"Oh," I fumbled, "I guess I had the wrong information." I turned to walk out of her office, which she was disassembling.

Sister Eleanor mellowed a bit and changed her tone of annoyance to one more business-like and asked me to sit for a minute.

"Did you know, Chris, that I was told that I won't be principal here next year?" she asked.

"Yes, I had heard from the ESL teachers," I answered.

"I'm so upset. Imagine, after all the work I've done here, I was just let go, with no reason. My mother and father are just terribly angry too," she explained.

It seemed odd to me for a woman in her forties to refer to her parents' reaction but I sympathized with her and reminded her that I, too, was experiencing unemployment problems. I had told Eleanor earlier in the year that my own position at the college was being changed to include more programming and I would have to reapply for it next year, with no promise of resecuring it.

"Oh, yes, but *this* is just so unfair," she continued with her own plight. "Imagine how hard it's been for me to finish this year, knowing I won't be returning." I listened a while longer as she vented her anger and realized that she was too absorbed in her own situation to recognize another. I finally left, thinking I had graduation plans all settled for Alejandro's big day.

"How do you feel about graduating?" I asked Alejandro.

"Oh, well, it's not such a big thing to me because they told me that I have to go to summer school or I can't really graduate," he answered.

"Really?" I said. I didn't think students could graduate conditionally but I encouraged Alejandro to enjoy the event despite the summer school commitment.

"A lot of other kids in my class have to go too, Chris. Almost all of us. Just a few of the smart kids, you know, like the girls I told you about. They don't have to go," continued Alejandro. We had given Carmen, the brightest girl in the class according to Alejandro, a ride home one snowy day after tutoring. Alejandro excitedly related that she was doing high school work already. "She brain," he said. I didn't understand so he repeated, "She brain, she smart," and he added, "she's real nice."

I remembered from the teacher interviews I did close to the school year's end that Alejandro's class was perceived as a weak one in general. Carmen and two other girls were the exceptions. Something seemed odd to me, to have to graduate a significant part of a 19-student class conditionally. I wondered how accurate Alejandro's perception was of the number of students forced to attend summer school.

Alma was annoyed about the summer school issue. "It's going to cost us $200 for 4 weeks of summer school. I think that's a lot, Christina. That's a lot of money for us." She also realized that it just took the wind out of her son's sails, so to speak, regarding his exuberance over graduation.

I was tempted to offer to enroll Alejandro in the summer school ESL program I knew of at a nearby school, which only cost $25 for 4 weeks. But I did not want to put Alma into a position of conflict with Sister Eleanor once again, who I feared would deny Alejandro graduation altogether if he did not jump through this last hoop she had required.

"I hate to see you have to pay that much money, Alma. But I think you're going to have to go along with Eleanor this time or she could withhold that diploma."

"You don't think he could just go to the ESL summer school again, Christina?" hinted Alma. "My husband and I just don't like those kids from his class and we really don't want him to be around them this summer. It's not just the money," she said. I still felt that Eleanor would never accept a substitute for her summer school demands. It was hard for me but I did not pursue the alternative summer school issue.

"I'm not paying yet. I'm going to see about this," Alma resolved. "Did Sister Eleanor give you a ticket for the graduation dinner, Christina?"

"No, she said I didn't need one. She said I could just come to the church on Saturday," I told Alma.

"Well, this is on Monday, I'm pretty sure. And I know it's a dinner for graduation and the tickets cost $10. I know; I talked to my *comadre*," Alma persisted. Alma was an expert at finding the expertise she needed in her community, at using "funds of knowledge" (Moll, 1992) available to her orally in compensation for what she could not access in writing. The *comadre* was the definitive fund of knowledge on Sorrowful Mother events and requirements. "I'm going to call the school today. I don't understand why they're not giving you the ticket. My husband and I really want you to be there," she said.

Alma called me later that day, very upset, and said that the secretary related her request for an extra ticket for me to Sister Eleanor. The principal sent a message back to Alma saying that she wanted only their own faculty to attend that dinner and would not sell her another ticket.

It had been difficult for me, all year, to get permission to visit classrooms at Sorrowful Mother. In the spring I had lost almost a month of school visits because of a serious illness that came upon me suddenly in April. I decided that nothing was going to stop me from attending this graduation dinner for Alejandro. It would be one of my last chances to observe him with his classmates. But more important, his parents wanted me there. To them, it was an honor to have a teacher take a special interest in their son and be visibly supportive of him. Alma and I finally pieced together our information, and I realized that this was a graduation awards dinner being held prior to the actual commencement in the church. I could not help but think that Eleanor had to have known which ticket I was after that day in her office when she told me that no tickets were needed. I wondered why she was so opposed to me attending the event. Alejandro's class was the first of our ESL groups to be graduating. The college's ESL program had been at Sorrowful Mother for 4 years.

Alma was furious. "She's not going to keep us from having you there. I just don't understand why she's acting like this. My husband is so upset. We've decided that we want you to take his ticket."

"Oh, no, I would never do that," I told Alma. "Your husband should be there with his son. I would never take his ticket."

"But we have two tickets; they're ours and we can do what we want to with them. My husband says he wants you there, no matter what we have to do. I know other families have brought guests before."

"Alma, I'll talk to Sister Eleanor again. I'll just tell her that I'll pay for a ticket myself for the dinner now that I know the date. Let me try once again," I said.

I must admit that it was with no small sigh of relief at not having to confront this woman, who seemed to conjure up every bit of Catholic cowardice I ever harbored, that I found Eleanor to be out of her office that day. I simply left a note on her desk requesting the ticket, with $10 enclosed.

Later that afternoon Sister Eleanor called me at home to say that they really did not have the supplies to make this dinner a large affair but that she would allow me to come because I had been involved in the school. The message about restricting it to their own faculty was not brought up. She was brusque; she had given in, but she clearly did so begrudgingly. I thanked her and reminded her that Alejandro and his class were the first students to be in the ESL program.

The evening of the dinner was stormy in more ways than one. A tornado and severe thunderstorm watch had just been issued on the television as I got ready to leave for Sorrowful Mother. As I drove my daughters to my husband's office to spend the evening, an ominous, dark cloud pursued us. The sky in the direction of Chicago and Sorrowful Mother was almost black.

As I drove east into the storm I was relieved that my children were not home alone. The sky looked so bad, and the wind began to whirl so strongly. By the time I got close to Sorrowful Mother, the rain was pounding on my car hood; the sky was greenish-gray. Long silver spears of lightening crackled above me and the thunder was deafening. As tree boughs dipped to sweep the streets and passing cars, I wondered if I had made a mistake in trying to attend this dinner. Even the weather seemed to be trying its best to keep me away. The neighborhood around Sorrowful Mother, which I had visited several times weekly all year, looked so different cast in the greenish-gray hues and covered with sheets of rain that I made a wrong turn and had to backtrack to the school. By the time I pulled into the school parking lot, the storm was lessening and the winds were calming, although the gray clouds still disguised the early hour of the June evening.

Mr. and Mrs. Juarez had saved a seat for me. Alejandro sat at a table in front reserved for the graduating class. Dressed in a black suit and starched white shirt he looked thin and serious, like a young, pre-occupied businessman. The Juarezes seemed nervous too; they spoke hardly at all to the other parents, who also seemed to be on formal, best behavior. Sister Eleanor and Mrs. Wright bustled around the crepe-paper adorned room, giving directives to the seventh graders and volunteer parents in attendance as helpers for the evening as intensely as if they were in charge of a presidential ball. This dimly lit, run-down school hall crisscrossed in crepe-paper, I realized, was Eleanor's kingdom. She supervised everything that was done, right down to the size the pieces of cake were cut into. And with no less rigor than the chief of staff at an executive press conference.

The Sorrowful Mother teachers and aides sat together at one table. It was obvious that this was a command performance; every staff member was there. All wore the traditional Mexican *copias*, small souvenir pins with embossed ribbons commemorating the event and date, which the seventh-grade girls pinned like a corsage to each guest's shirt or dress as they entered.

I chatted with the Juarezes until the ceremony began. Mr. Juarez sat with his arms folded across his chest at the end of the table, looking tired and tense.

"Did she say hello to you, Christina?" asked Alma.

"Yes. She acknowledged me when I entered, but walked right away," I said. "I don't know, Alma; I think she's just mad at the world right now because of her job loss. The only other thing I can think of is that she's mad because one of our ESL teachers was sick a lot a while ago and she hates when teachers are absent repeatedly."

But Alma always wondered, really worried, that Sister Eleanor begrudged her family the attention they received from me. "I don't think she thinks I deserve your help for my son. There are better families who need help, I know," Alma would say. My help gnawed at her, yet she vacillated between feeling guilty and undeserving to feeling angry that Eleanor clearly did not favor her family as she did her *comadre's* and certain others. Alma introduced me to her special friend that evening.

It was the first time I saw the *comadre* about whom I had heard so much. It was easy to see why Sister Eleanor liked this family and allowed the *comadre* to tutor children in groups at the school. The *comadre's* volunteer help in reading to Alejandro and other students had even been given priority over his remedial reading teacher's class time until Ms. Gonzales complained about the conflict in schedules. She was an attractive *Tejana* [Texan of Mexican descent] with shiny black hair falling over her shoulders. She wore a wide-legged black pants suit that flowed to the floor. Her son, dressed in black pants and a formal white shirt with gold embroidered designs and a matching gold bow tie, politely came over to our table to shake hands with Mr. and Mrs. Juarez.

The *comadre* had it all together; she was poised and confident; she directed the seventh-grade helpers as adeptly as Eleanor did, and her children appeared well-mannered and respectful. The irony of it was that, according to Alejandro, the *comadre's* son in seventh grade was already dabbling in drugs and had had a falling out with Alejandro for not joining in with him. He also had "ideas" about girls, as Alejandro put it, which Alejandro did not agree with at all. Alejandro had confided in me and his mother about this but I doubt that the *comadre* or Sister Eleanor would ever have guessed what was going on in this prized family.

The program began and the pastor, a young blond-haired man who spoke Spanish quite well though laboriously, welcomed the guests. He also gave credit to Sister Eleanor for organizing the evening, which was to include an hour of live music by a Mexican band, *El Cielo y las Estrellas* [The Sky and the Stars], as a special treat arranged by the principal. "This is the priest who told Sister Eleanor she could not return," I whispered to Alma and her husband. "It must be hard for her to sit with him this evening."

Surprisingly, Father Smith's address was the last time Spanish would be used during the formal program that evening. As Sister Eleanor began to call out the various awards, I wondered why she did not explain anything in Spanish, which she spoke well though not with native fluency.

There were many awards. The typical academic achievement awards were announced by Eleanor and certificates were passed out by Mrs. Wright. Carmen and two other girls won most of those. Other categories revolved around service, responsibility, and class participation. Even John, the class cut-up, received an award for giving the gift of laughter. Everyone had received something except Alejandro. I waited and waited to hear his name, particularly when certificates were given to the group of boys (of whom Alejandro was one) who cleaned and emptied the trash daily since the school had no janitor. His name was left out of that group, too.

Finally, at the end of the awards, several names were called for a category described as "always getting a job assigned done," and Alejandro was named. I breathed a sigh of relief; at least he had one certificate, although most of his classmates had several. Alejandro accepted it solemnly. Mr. and Mrs. Juarez applauded loudly. Within minutes, the physical education teacher's awards for the presidential fitness exams were announced, and Alejandro was named once again. Alma smiled proudly. I translated each award's significance briefly for the Juarezes since they did not understand much of the proceedings. "Christina," Alma leaned over to me, "the kids who got a lot of diplomas, are they the best students?"

I explained that these weren't the diplomas. Those would be given at the actual graduation ceremony on Saturday. These were awards given by the school. Alma looked confused.

I could see that the strain of trying to comprehend English all evening after working all day was taxing for both of Alejandro's parents. They went through the motions of applauding but gazed off and appeared to "turn off" the linguistic demands.

Sister Eleanor proceeded to announce that she had a small token of appreciation to present to the parents of the graduates who had sacrificed greatly to send their children to Sorrowful Mother. She was keenly aware of the monetary strain a private education entailed, yet not completely sympathetic when tuition demands necessitated transferring students to public schools. I suspected that the Juarezes' defection to Shepherd with their younger children was part of the reason they had fallen from grace with Eleanor. She began to call parents to the front of the room, beginning with the Juarezes. Neither moved toward her. Oh, God, I thought. What should I do? Everyone turned their heads to our table; there was an awkward gap in activity and speech. Obviously, Mr. and Mrs. Juarez had no idea of what was going on and just sat. I leaned over to Mr. Juarez, who was closer to me, and said quickly, "She's calling you to go up front."

When Alma saw Alejandro, Sr. rise, she got up and started after him. She had a terrified expression on her face. By then, Alejandro, Sr. had reached the front and was handed a card by Eleanor. Mrs. Wright offered her hand to shake, and Alejandro, Sr. figured out that this was all he had to do, as the next family was called. Alma returned to the table lowering her head.

"I wasn't listening and neither were you," Alejandro, Sr. said softly to Alma as he sat down and shook his head embarrassedly. They had been given a card with their son's graduation picture printed on it. I commented on how nice a remembrance it was and wished again that Eleanor had used her Spanish that evening and saved us all from an embarrassing moment.

After the awards, each table was directed one by one to the buffet dinner. The graduates went first. Alejandro seemed subdued and did not look in our direction at all. When it was our group's turn, Mr. Juarez would not go to the buffet. He told me that his stomach was bothering him.

Alma whispered to me, "He's so upset with Sister Eleanor that he said he won't eat here. He thinks it's disgraceful how she acted about you and especially about the extra ticket for this dinner."

"Please join us," I coaxed Mr. Juarez. Alma said, "Come, just have some salad, something." Reluctantly he rose and joined us in line. Although he put a few things on his plate he barely ate a morsel. For Alejandro, Sr., it was his small silent protest for the mistreatment of his wife, his son, and his son's teacher at the hands of the formidable figure of Sister Eleanor. I thought of a children's book I read to my daughter, *Ming Lo Moves the Mountain* (Lobel, 1982), in which a small man and his wife attempted to move a large mountain that overshadowed their house. "They loved their house," it said, "but they did not love the mountain" (p. 21). Alma and Alejandro were devoted to their faith. They loved their religious tradition. But they did not love the embodiment of it that Eleanor represented. Yet to Alejandro, she must have seemed no less immovable an obstacle than Ming Lo's mountain. Both men, though small in stature, found a way to confront their problems, and both Sister Eleanor and the mountain were oblivious to their struggle. Yet, I felt that in some small way Mr. Juarez, by refusing to break bread at the celebration, felt vindicated for the wrongs his "mountain" had subjected him to that evening.

During the dinner, the band hired by Sister Eleanor played loudly, their lead singer coming close to being on key only at times. A second singer joined her and they rendered some dramatic romantic duets together, each feigning heartache.

After everyone finished eating, *El Cielo y las Estrellas* left, reluctantly. Their lead singer, a middle-aged Mexican woman who led the traditional ballads and polkas they sang, made a valiant attempt to convince the *directora* [person in charge] to pay them to play longer. Eleanor ignored the cajoling and *Las Estrellas* packed away their instruments as their leaders passed out business cards and flyers advertising their next appearance. The Juarezes laughed at the group's persistence and Alma made a clever joke about the *estrellas* failing to shine that night.

A D.J. with a sound system then set up and tables were quickly taken down to make room for the eighth-grade dance, which immediately followed the ceremony. Alejandro left his peers and approached his parents with a sullen look on his face. A storm of another kind was brewing between Alejandro and his parents of which I was oblivious until that moment.

Parents were invited to stay for the dance or to return in 2 hours for their children, who would be chaperoned by the teachers and Eleanor. The evening was a wonderful gift to the eighth graders. But Alma had decided that her son could not stay alone at the dance. It was clearly Alma's decision. I mistook this for her reluctance to have her husband drive back for him from Brighton Park and offered to drive her home to her younger children, who were staying with an aunt. Alejandro, Jr. looked visibly upset even by the suggested compromise. I began to realize that the solemn face he wore all evening had nothing to do with awards or graduating.

"They don't trust me to stay at the dance alone," he complained.

"We'll wait for a while and you can dance a couple of dances," said Alma. "I don't want to leave him, Christina," she replied to my offer.

Her son pouted openly. I had never seen Alejandro act like this before. His *comadre* approached him during this time, embraced him, and gave him a large card.

"Open it while I'm here, Alejandro," she said excitedly. He opened it listlessly and just murmured, "Thanks," for a card generously filled with money. Alma, smiling, gave him a small gold box, which he also opened with disinterest. In it was a beautiful gold cross.

"Your mother always wanted you to have something like that," his *comadre* commented. "Put it on, it's beautiful."

Alma helped him hang the glistening crucifix around his neck. She looked so pleased with her gift. But Alejandro, immersed in his quest for permission to remain alone at the dance, reacted emotionlessly to this special moment in his mother's eyes.

The *comadre* left and there were more short verbal exchanges between Alejandro and his mother, plaintive looks toward his father, who remained quiet. He wanted to stay alone at the dance; she did not approve of him remaining there without a parent. For a moment I thought Alma was teasing her son as she often did before she gave permission for something he desired. But I was wrong.

"You're really not going to let him stay?" I asked her. "This is his graduation dance and your *comadre* and the teachers are all here. All of the students are staying; it would be nice if he could too," I said.

"He can stay for a while," replied Alma. "I don't want to leave the other children alone until 10:30." Apparently, it was out of the question for her to leave Alejandro alone at the dance.

Alejandro whined about her decision, loud music already played, the lights were dimmed.

"Look, Alejandro," snapped Alma. "You have your choice—you can go home with us right now or you can stay for a half hour and we'll wait here. That's it!" Alma asserted her parental power definitively, in the middle of the eighth-grade dance, and did not waver in her decision.

I quickly said my good-byes and left. Alma sent her husband to walk with me to my car. Alejandro, Jr. barely acknowledged my departure. I felt badly for all of them that this special evening was ending so stressfully.

In the parking lot Mr. Juarez explained that they had had some problems with Alejandro the day before and for this reason his wife was so adamantly against him staying alone at the dance. He was supposed to return home right after school the day before to watch the younger children but was hours late. He had stopped at a friend's house and lost track of time while playing Nintendo. By then, traffic was bad and the buses were slow, which delayed him even further. Alejandro, Sr. and Alma had no idea where he was or what was going on all afternoon and were calling from work.

"We're so worried about him, Christina. We don't like the kids he hangs around with. And he's always on the phone when he's home. There's a girl who calls him 8, 9, 10 times each night," said Mr. Juarez.

"Well, I think he needs something to do over the summer," I ventured. "I think he gets bored being in the house all the time. It's a hard age. He's not old enough to work a little somewhere and there's no summer sports program near your home for him, is there?" I asked.

"No, nothing. We have Ricardo on a baseball team but there's nothing for the older boys. I'm going to stop my second job in a couple of weeks. Even though we need the money, I know we need to be around more for our children. That's more important. Alma is trying to switch to the day shift, too, so that at least we can all be together in the evening. I want to do things with him, go to a lake, or the pool, or something. I'm so afraid of what's happening with him," Mr. Juarez confided in me.

It was his "I'll be your best friend" philosophy again. I had rarely seen parents so protective of a child, so afraid of peers. But then, when I thought more about it, I remembered other Mexican families in Chicago I had known over the years who sent their children back to Mexico for high school—so great was their fear of gangs and violence in their neighborhood. Others kept daughters with them constantly, getting them involved in school programs, teaching them crafts they had learned in Mexico. A close Mexican friend and co-worker of my own who lived in a Latino neighborhood in Chicago had her son and daughter involved in a Mexican folklore dance company in the neighborhood and church activities.

"It doesn't matter to me what it is that we do," said my friend Maria, "as long as we're together as a family. My husband likes the dance group; he helps out with the music. I'm so glad."

The problem I saw for Alejandro was that his parents, though faithful churchgoers, did not get involved in church activities. Their parish, still headed largely by Slavic members, was not as active in the Latino community as some on the west side. And Sorrowful Mother did not have the funds to run after-school or summer programs other than remedial ones. The attitude pervading their summer school was a remedial one, not one of providing summer enrichment activities. By and large, from what I observed over the years, Mexican parents did not seek out library, YMCA, or other community-based programs due to fears of English language demands, lack of knowledge about them, and a reluctance to send children outside of the family for entertainment. The summer promised to be a long one for Alejandro, I feared.

After that stormy evening, I talked to Alejandro about his certificates, gifts, and the dance.

"What are you planning to do with your graduation money, Alejandro?" I asked. I, too, had given him a card with money for him to choose a present for himself. "I hope you get something you really like. I wanted to pick something out for you but I didn't know what you'd enjoy most."

"Oh, I spent it already, Chris," he answered, grinning, and I was surprised.

"Did you get something you really like?" I asked him.

"Well, I got my dad this really nice jacket, for Father's Day. It looks like leather. It's really nice."

"You spent your graduation money on your father?" I asked incredulously.

"Yeah, Chris. I wanted to. My mother said she'd pay me back when she gets her next check, but I told her not to. I gave my little brother money for his class trip, too. He needed $5 and my mother was looking all around the house for it and I said, 'Here, Ricky, I'll take care of it.'" Alejandro looked so pleased to have been able to do these things.

It was not the first time that I had seen Alejandro's actions speak louder than his words. His was a truly kind heart. When he realized, for example, that his writing in his journal was important to me as part of my study and again when I was ill, he wrote longer, more thoughtful entries than he had all year long. He did for me what was the most difficult thing for him to do—he wrote.

"You know, I never saw you so upset with your mother as you were the night of the class dance, Alejandro," I said.

"No, Chris, no, I was okay," he insisted. "You know, I got to stay for the whole dance. My parents waited the whole time anyway."

"Oh, that's good Alejandro," I said. "I wanted you to be able to stay for that dance. I was surprised at your mother; she really was strict with you. But you know, you didn't thank her for that beautiful gift. She was so happy to give that to you," I added.

"Yeah, Chris. I told her later," he said. "You know, I told them, 'Yo soy un good boy' ['I'm a good boy']. They don't have to worry so much."

A few days later, at his graduation, Alejandro teased Alma and his dad about that evening. "You know, Chris, estaban echándome dirty looks [they were giving me dirty looks] all night long but I'm a good boy. I don't do nothin' wrong, I told them. Really, yo soy un good boy!" he insisted.

Swan Songs

To see a child is to see a possibility, someone in the process of becoming.
—*The Tact of Teaching*, M. van Manen

I had never been inside Sorrowful Mother church. I walked into the large old building the morning of Alejandro's graduation for the first time. It was beautiful. The huge original altar and the paneled sanctuary that surrounded it were sepia-toned wood that glowed warmly in the candlelight. Large, intricately carved statues of biblical scenes were recessed into pale pink, softly lit semicircular alcoves at both ends of the front walls. Gold embossed Slavic prayers and saints' names, glistening anomalies, were lettered under the paintings and shrines, traces of past congregations. A banner depicting the Mexican Blessed Mother hung at the side of the altar in recognition of the new audience the aging church now served.

Mr. Juarez sat in a pew by himself at the far side of the church, looking small under the high-reaching cathedral ceiling. My family and I headed toward him. He held his forehead with his hands. The moment he saw us he stood and began shaking our hands and guiding us into his row. It was then that I saw Alma returning from the front of the church and the direction of Sister Eleanor, looking distressed. She sat in the pew in front of us. I wanted to make room for her in our row so that she and her husband could be together, but she and Mr. Juarez insisted that we stay where we were.

"Christina, I'm so upset with Sister Eleanor," Alma whispered. The ceremony had not yet begun, the small choir was assembling, more guests were still arriving.

"What happened?" I asked.

"She called me last night and said that she was not going to let Alejandro graduate today because I haven't paid the $200 for summer school yet. Can you imagine! She called me on a Friday night to say that if she didn't have the money the next day, my son couldn't get his diploma with his class."

"Oh, Alma," I said, "can I lend you the money just so you can straighten all of this out?"

"Oh, no, Christina. I'm not paying today. I can get the money. I told her not to worry, that she would get her money when he came to summer school on Monday. How am I supposed to get to the bank on a Friday night? She can wait until Monday for that money. I'll work on getting it together over the weekend," she said determinedly. "She just turned around and walked away from me in front of the church," Alma sighed.

Within moments, Mrs. Lago, Alejandro's computer teacher who spoke Spanish, came over to Alma's pew.

"It'll be okay, Mrs. Juarez," she whispered. "Just be sure to bring the money on Monday and she'll be satisfied." She glanced toward Sister Eleanor, who was ordering the choir here and there. "Just don't get involved with her now. I talked to her. I said I'd take care of it. Today's her last day as principal. She won't have anything to do with summer school. After today, she has no more control of anything in the school," she explained in Spanish.

Mrs. Juarez assured her that she'd have the money by then and told her how upset Sister Eleanor had gotten her. "She just walked away from me," Alma said.

"I know, I know," she said sympathetically and glanced at me. "Everything's gonna be alright. I told her I'd take care of things with you." Mr. Juarez just looked down at the floor during the whole exchange.

Right up to the last moment of Alejandro's time at Sorrowful Mother, literally the last moment before his graduation, his educational fate hung precariously in the wind due to the flexing of muscle by a woman labeled a "religious" by the Catholic Church. This is a special category according to church officials; its members are set apart from mere "lay" people who do not dedicate their whole lives to the service of God. Sister Eleanor bustled around the front of the church, her eyes avoiding the little segment of her school's community that sat in the side pews, reeling from her bureaucratic pronouncement that morning. I could not help but think how far from my conception of service in God's name was Eleanor's treatment of the Juarezes that morning.

Pomp and Circumstance began shakily by the organist, and the first of the burgundy-robed graduates marched down the long aisle. I scanned the many bronze faces with black crops of hair peeking from under maroon mortar boards, holding my breath until I recognized

Alejandro toward the end of the line. He had made it—despite threats
of low grades, low effort, and summer school bills, and, sadly, despite
his school principal. Alejandro was going to graduate on a gorgeous,
warm, sunny spring morning in June.

He appeared somber, intent upon following the ceremonial directions perfectly as each pair of graduates marched a predetermined
space apart from each other. The graduation mass was uneventful save
for the priest's sermon in which he officially bid farewell to Sister
Eleanor and presented her with a wrapped gift box. Eleanor accepted
the box gravely; her face remained expressionless. I felt that she was
seething with anger. She did not make eye contact with Father Smith
at all.

After mass, the graduates received their diplomas. Alejandro was
still seriously following the directions Mrs. Wright had drilled during
weeks of practice for this day and solemnly accepted his long-awaited
document. The graduating class then came to the front of the church
and read farewells and thank yous they had written as a group tribute
to their school and to Sister Eleanor.

During the recitation of this group farewell, the class stood in
prescribed positions in front of the altar, each moving very quietly to
one of several microphones for the reading. Only two students read in
Spanish. One of them began delivering his long piece nervously and
almost inaudibly, speaking into the side of the microphone. Realizing
he could not be heard, Alejandro very unobtrusively reached back and
moved the microphone toward his friend's mouth, never leaving his
own spot in the configuration, his friend never pausing in his lines.
Thanks to Alejandro's quick thinking, his friend's long tribute in his
native language to Sorrowful Mother School could then be heard perfectly by the predominantly Spanish-speaking audience.

I saw Mrs. Wright's hand in many of the student's statements,
including Alejandro's. "Thank you for our wonderful teachers who
work so hard," I heard over and over again with slight variations. Yet
one girl was moved to tears as she mentioned Sister Eleanor's departure. It was Julie, who had played Mary at the boisterous Stations of
the Cross religion class. I was surprised. In classes she often volunteered
sarcastic remarks and negative comments about teachers, kids, Sister
Eleanor, and schooling in general. Perhaps overall emotions were running high that day, or the desire to sympathize with Eleanor's plight
became contagious among the eighth graders, or she truly felt sorry
for their fallen leader. It was hard for me to muster genuine compassion or even to see it emerge for this administrator who had just minutes earlier treated one of her "charges" so coldly.

After the ceremony, the graduates and their families and friends gathered in the school parking lot excitedly congratulating their loved ones and taking pictures. Many of the students were in tears by this time; Alejandro's best friend was weeping openly and laughing at himself. Alejandro remained composed and a little ill at ease. I had asked my husband to take whatever poses Alma wanted with our camera because I knew the Juarezes did not have one. Hesitantly at first, but soon with more assertion, Alma asked for shots of her family, my family, and the *comadre* with her son. Alejandro asked for only two pictures: one with his cousins and the other with his closest friend, Juan, still in tears. Eleanor and Mrs. Wright posed for many pictures with eighth graders. But I could see that Alma was keeping her distance from the principal, monitoring her whereabouts by periodically glancing in her direction, keeping her clan far from that end of the crowd. I asked Mr. and Mrs. Juarez if they wanted a picture with Father Smith, who had baptized most of the Juarez children. Alma said yes but was apprehensive about requesting it. Once we motioned him over to the little corner we stood in, she asked for several photos and just beamed as Father Smith graciously posed and chatted with all of us, thanking me for the ESL program at the school. I was grateful for his friendly response to us and his acknowledgment of the program, which was left unmentioned in Sister Eleanor's long list of thanks and farewells inside. It had become apparent, I felt, that we were the only group not approaching the sniffling Sister Eleanor and the imperturbable Mrs. Wright, who at this point escorted Sister Eleanor among the crowd, arm in arm with her. Despite my disappointment in Eleanor's treatment of the Juarezes, I was glad Mrs. Wright was there to console and help her through this difficult final function as principal. This was truly Eleanor's swan song.

"Christina," Alma called as we walked toward our cars after the event. "Did Alejandro read his part well during the graduation? I get so nervous when he has to do something like that." The insecurity of their problem with reading always hung over their heads.

"Oh, yes, he did just fine and wasn't that great of him to fix the microphone so quickly?" I responded.

"Oh, I noticed that!" said Alma. "You know Christina, I thought to myself, every once in a while my son is really intelligent, *muy inteligente*, not always, *pero de vez en cuando*" [very intelligent, not always, but once in a while], she laughed and looked proudly in Alejandro's direction. By this time he had an assortment of graduation balloons to add to the one his oldest sister brought along for him. Several neighborhood girls had slipped into the back of the church with them and presented the balloons and some gifts to him outside. A petite attractive seventh grader from Sorrowful Mother stood in the center of the other girls. She was the one who called him every night on the phone, Alma pointed out. Angie, her name I was told, brought Alejandro a beautiful gold ring with his initials. Alejandro insisted that she was not his girlfriend and just barely betrayed any emotion toward her as she and her friends fluttered about him. This was the first time that Angie had brought her attention to Alejandro out into the open for his parents to see. Obviously, Alejandro was not going to get into trouble with his parents and remained very subdued. He was going to prove his "good boy" protestations and was on his best behavior.

Alma invited my family to join them for a celebratory lunch. She suggested two restaurants and asked my husband and me to decide which we would prefer.

"Oh, this is Alejandro's day and yours," I told her. "All of you should decide."

"No," she insisted. "My husband and I want you to choose. You've done so much for our son and we've wanted to take you and your family out to dinner for a long time. Please, which would you prefer? Which is better for you, Christina?" The Juarezes knew I had been hospitalized the month before for stomach problems and had been very warmly concerned over my health, even sending food for my family when I first came home from the hospital and could not yet walk much.

I felt quite sure that the younger children would enjoy the pizza parlor they had mentioned rather than a sit-down full dinner restaurant, which was the other suggestion. Also, I was sure it would not be as expensive. So we headed to a favorite local Italian restaurant specializing in Chicago style deep dish pizza.

To my surprise and her son's shock, Alma invited Angie and her three friends to join us and even agreed to pick them up at their respective homes so that they could tell their parents. Alma flashed a look of concern to Alejandro and directed everyone as to where to sit and in which car to ride as they left to pick up the girls.

"I'm a good boy, she doesn't have to worry," Alejandro said as we divided the younger children between their car and our own. "They were giving me dirty looks at the dance too and they saw that I was good there. *Yo soy un good boy*, really!" he continued his familiar reminder.

When we arrived at the restaurant I smiled and said quietly to Alejandro, "I can't believe your mother let these girls come. I know she doesn't approve of them calling you so much."

"Yeah, Chris. I was surprised! I couldn't hardly believe it either," he said softly.

The younger children had a wonderful time at the restaurant, which included a game room where they played until the many pizzas Alma and Alejandro, Sr. ordered were ready. Their newly graduated son beamed at the end of the table, sipping soda with the girls, but on best, reserved behavior. Mr. Juarez smiled a lot that afternoon and seemed less preoccupied than usual. My children thoroughly and visibly enjoyed the lunch and the games, which made Mr. and Mrs. Juarez so happy for they always worried if their choice in food agreed with my family's taste. "This is like a dream come true for my daughter Mary," I said. "She's never played so many games before. She just loves it." Mr. Juarez and my husband supplied a steady stream of quarters to all the kids. It was truly a lovely lunch, a relaxed, enjoyable way to end a day that had such a stressful start with the threat that Alejandro's graduation would not take place.

"Do you think I did something wrong, Christina? Maybe I shouldn't have let those girls come along," Alma leaned and whispered to me at our end of the table.

"Oh, no, Alma," I said. "I think it was really nice of you to invite them. This is Alejandro's day and he should be able to share it with some friends."

"That's what I thought," said Alma. "This *is* a special day."

Fading Dreams, Enduring Hope

> Multiple interpretations constitute multiple realities; the "common" itself
> becomes multiplex and endlessly challenging, as each person reaches out
> from his/her own ground toward what might be, should be, is not yet.
> —*The Dialectic of Freedom*, M. Greene

As Alejandro reached out from his own ground, what was it that he
tried to grasp? As a Mexican-American minority of limited English
proficiency, will he be confronted with "the wall" that Langston Hughes
(1968) described in the following poem?

> It was a long time ago.
> I have almost forgotten my dream.
> But it was there then,
> In front of me,
> Bright as a sun—
> My dream.
> And then the wall rose,
> Rose slowly,
> Slowly,
> Between me and my dream.
> Rose slowly, slowly
> Dimming,
> Hiding,
> The light of my dream
> Rose until it touched the sky. (p. 426)

Maxine Greene, who cited Langston Hughes's poem, wrote of her
conviction that we who are in education cannot know, cannot truly
know how it was, how it is, ". . . we cannot truly understand the walls
immigrants and minorities face. But we can attend to some of the voices,
some of the stories" (1988, pp. 88–89).

118

In attending to Alejandro's story, a young man emerges who wishes for economic success, and blue eyes.

"I wish I had blue eyes," he said one summer day as we walked along Lake Michigan. "Blue eyes are the best."

"Yeah," laughed his oldest sister. "He really wants blue eyes."

"I wanna get a nice, you know, a good job," he says, "to work downtown or maybe as a carpenter. I'll probably go to college, like just for 2 years, they're too expensive. I wanna get married but like when I'm 21 to 23. . . . Yeah, I wanna be a dad some day."

The dreams are vague but they are his, rooted in the ground that a strong family of inimitable faith has tilled and turned. Implicit to their realization is the need for English literacy. When he was younger, his mother recalled, Alejandro talked about wanting to be a doctor or a lawyer. She was clearly proud of those aspirations. As time went on, Alma began to question the schooling demands of such professions, began to suspect that perhaps it was already too late to hope that her son could realistically pursue those vocations. During his eighth-grade year, Alejandro himself began to pare down his career goals, and I found it difficult to discourage the direction he was taking. As realities of academic challenges settle in, he has already scaled down his dreams of employment to that of an office worker.

Alma, too, was vague about her hopes for Alejandro's future. "We've been so fortunate, people have helped us out so much. I'd like to see Alejandro do something where he could help people. I don't know what, but I think it would be nice for him to help other people." She recognized with disappointment that, due to his academic challenges and their monetary reality, this helping profession she envisioned will not likely be medicine or law. However, as is typical of Alma, she switched gears and focused on realistic alternatives. "I want him to continue going to school, I know," she gazed wistfully out her living room windows as we talked. "My husband and I tell him all the time to take advantage of the opportunity of going to school. We didn't have a chance to and it holds us back."

What Alma and her husband were very clear on is what they do not hope for their son. "We don't want him to end up in jobs like we have, bad factory jobs. We're held back because we can't fill out forms, we can't get promoted like other people we see, we don't know enough English. We work and work and never earn much."

Their aspirations for their son in terms of employment and education get translated into constant social restraints for Alejandro. Alma related their warnings to Alejandro not to think about marriage until his mid-twenties, when school is done and he has a good job.

"Some day he's going to realize that I was only 16 when I got married and here I'm telling him he can't even date till he's 18 or think of getting married till he's 24 or 25. I've always lied to the kids about the date of our marriage but now they're starting to realize how old I am and how old they are. They're figuring it out," Alma grins. But she is adamant that her son will not marry at an early age like she did.

"You know, Christina, Alejandro is very innocent," she told me one morning as we drove together to the social security office to investigate special educational allotments for her oldest daughter's vision and learning problems. "Last week my sister and I were talking and cooking in the kitchen and Alejandro asked why he felt sweaty and funny when a girl in his class touched his ears and neck. He was very serious, Christina, poor thing. My sister and I tried to keep a straight face. He went on to describe how odd he felt, how he had butterflies in his stomach, you know. He's very naive, very innocent about things between girls and boys."

"I think you and your husband need to talk to him about those things, don't you?" I asked.

"Oh, yes, yes. I told my husband that he had to sit down and have a 'facts of life' talk with him. And he did. He told Alejandro that's how it starts. You start touching a girl's face and one thing leads to another and you have babies. He told him he shouldn't date until he's older, at least 18."

"But I don't think he really understands how everything happens. Alma, I think he needs to know. He's almost 14, right?"

Alma agreed but it was clear that neither she nor her husband would frankly explain sexual intercourse to their son. It was out of the question. He would receive a healthy dose of Catholic taboos surrounding "it" and admonitions to avoid "it," but to discuss "it" openly or scientifically was asking them to do something culturally inappropriate. Their focus would be a moral one.

"I tease Alejandro because he's told me he doesn't like dark hair, you know, like mine. I say, 'So you're not going to look for a girl like your Mom to marry?' But he has always liked blond hair. I told him, 'Then that means you're not going to marry a Mexican?'" she laughs. Despite the good-natured teasing about his preference in looks and his emerging ability to dance at family parties and events like *quinceaños* [15-year-olds' coming-out parties], he is closely monitored to keep things on a friendly, casual basis with girls.

"There are two *güeras* [Anglo girls] in the neighborhood who have noticed Alejandro. When he and his father are cutting the grass they walk by the house again and again. My husband tells Alejandro he should be friendly and chat with them. He tells him he should chat with your daughter, too. It would help his English," she smiles. "He's just too shy, he's embarrassed about his English."

A 14-year-old Mexican-American boy, who finds that girls like his looks yet who doesn't quite understand what to do about it, emerged from the 10-year-old I once tutored. He still struggled to read and write in English, preferred blond hair and blue eyes (obviously picking up society's biased preferences through the T.V. shows and movies he so loves), and was kept bonded closely to his family in order to resist peer influences upon him. He did not particularly like Mexico, felt more comfortable in his old "hood" than his new, prettier, cleaner, safer (at least for Caucasians) neighborhood of Brighton Park, and was frightened at the prospect of attending a large urban high school.

"I miss Sorrowful Mother," he told me that summer, "but not the teachers; not Mrs. Wright. I have friends at school *only*, you know. We did lots of things together. I mean now we're gonna start all over. I mean none of my friends are gonna come (to Crown High School). I'm gonna feel like, how you say, embarrassed?"

"Why will you feel embarrassed?" I asked Alejandro.

"Well, cause I don't even know the people that go there." I remembered the relief I saw in Alejandro's face almost a year ago when Shepherd Elementary School could not take him into their overcrowded eighth grade and he had the chance to go back into the arms of Sorrowful Mother. He most likely will be reprieved as well from attending the high school he fears, for at least a while. Sara called to tell me that with fiscal problems being what they are at the Chicago Board of Education, she strongly doubts that Crown will open on time in September. She suggested enrolling Alejandro in the college's tutoring program in the fall for double sessions so that he could keep up on some type of work with his reading and writing. This tutoring was already promised in the petitioning process for Alejandro's acceptance into Crown, in addition to an updated educational evaluation during the summer.

The summer provided a more relaxed context for me to share time with Alejandro. I learned a lot observing him out of his classroom. The burden of terrifically difficult homework was lifted from our relationship, at least temporarily. The Juarez children, my daughters, and I wandered through zoos, museums, and parks together. Alejandro teased me about my "field trips," as he called them, and is finally comfortable enough with me to express his own opinions, though still cautiously.

"I don't like museums so much," he grinned. "Why don't we go to the movies instead? I like going to the movies."

"Well, I promised my younger daughter we'd go to the aquarium and the Field Museum today, but next week we'll go to a movie, okay?" I suggested.

"Oh, yeah! I wanna see *My Boyfriend's Back*," he said.

"*My Boyfriend's Back?* Isn't that the one where someone returns from the dead?" I asked.

"Oh, yeah, Chris. It looks good. Don't worry!" he laughed.

As we drove to and from his weekly diagnostic evaluations this summer and on our "field trips" Alejandro brought along tapes he had recorded from the radio. He told me the categories of music each group plays. "This is techno, Chris, and this one, this is plain rap." Some have a Latin beat but all have lyrics in English. He subvocalized all the words from the songs and could decipher hard-to-understand lines for me. This from a student who could not remember how to spell three-letter, primary-level words in school.

"He listens to his music all day," said Alicia, his oldest sister. "That's all he does any more."

"Yeah," he laughed. "I don't even watch no T.V. much any more," Alejandro added. "I haven't been out all week since the detectives," he referred to the incident when his cousin unknowingly wore a cap backwards as they played basketball in their alley and was accosted by two Chicago detectives.

Is it the repetition, I wondered? Is it the rhythm that could be helping him to memorize, to comprehend line after line of songs packed with English words? Or is it the meaning these tapes hold for him? They are esteemed by his peers with whom he talks on the phone, tape player at one ear, phone receiver at the other.

I also have watched Alejandro carefully during my field trips that summer and although he often began disinterestedly, he readily joined in activities that are hands-on. At both the zoo and the Field Museum he perked up when exhibits had buttons to push, flaps to open, sounds to hear. He approached them with the same enthusiasm as his younger brother, Ricardo, who is a bright, animated, adventurous learner. But Alejandro did not attempt to use reading to gain information about what he was experiencing, not even single-word labels.

"What's this?" he would ask, completely ignoring the sign next to the button he had just pushed at the zoo's African exhibit. There he had to analyze simple clues to figure out situations in the wild. Integrating the clues seemed beyond him as the younger children excitedly explained answers to him. At the museum I pointed out that the word next to a button he quickly pressed named the animal in the scene in front of him that made the sound he heard. I pointed to the label next to the button "grouse" and the matching label near the stuffed grouse in the scene. Alejandro had a "light bulb over the head" reaction. His face lit up as he suddenly grasped a totally new concept. His reading teacher spoke of the same type of reaction she would notice when, clearly, meaning broke through for him as they discussed a reading topic he had initially decoded successfully but with no comprehension.

"I know he can learn," said Ms. Gonzales. "I've seen his expression change and his whole face light up and I know, he's got it now. He understands. But he has to be pushed to do it. If I had him more for reading that's what I would do with him. Really go through the material . . . make connections and make him think about it."

I saw the need for that "push" this summer too. Alejandro preferred the safe, the comfortable, like his world of tapes. Although he never refused to come on our "field trips" and has even declined my offer to bring along a friend of his, he would rather do something more familiar to him. He spoke of being bored by things he used to like to do with his family and often faced his days with lassitude, not expressing interest in the world around him. Yet, he seemed to value the time we spend together.

"I don't want to ask a friend to come," he told me clearly one day. "I'm goin' out to be with you, not with a friend." When we talked on the phone to make arrangements for our outings, he enjoyed long conversations, relating his family's activities, his plans, even asking me to listen to a song he's taped that he thinks I'll like. Although I had to coax him to read the books I found for him that summer, he offered to chat, to clean, to cut grass, to do other things he feels more competent in.

"But I want you to read, Alejandro, not to cut my grass," I told him.

"I'm gonna do it, really, Chris. I like the book. I've kind of, ya know, gotten into it. It's a good story, like a mystery." I was encouraged as he related details of a new book I bought him, written by a local author who set out to compose an interesting book series for middle-grade to junior high students with reading difficulties.

"I've been busy 'cause I cleaned my father's car, all day. I really did. Then he took me to Dunkin' Donuts. And tomorrow we have to go to my cousin's wedding," he explained. I saw more clearly as well that summer how narrow his world of experience is. Alejandro would not go swimming with me and my family this summer. Neither would Alicia, Almita, or Ricardo. Only his younger sister Lupita would venture into the 3-foot children's pool. Alicia, Almita, and Ricardo said they were afraid. Alejandro said he just didn't like swimming. They all still cringed at my pet cat if they even caught a glimpse of him in another room. Alejandro's parents have managed to negotiate at Dunkin' Donuts, which is a treat for their children. Lack of English and low textual literacy have restricted the family's willingness to try new stores, restaurants, or amusements. His parents hear about things within their social network but are very cautious to attempt things that move them outside of their family and Spanish-speaking friends, and with good reason. For it is not only linguistic fears that limit them; neighborhood gang activity is always a concern.

Not long after graduation, Alma related a terrifying incident to me revolving around a family outing not far from their home. After shopping, she and her sister's family stopped at a nearby McDonald's to eat. Apparently a gang that dominated the restaurant came and encircled the entire Juarez table, staring at them, arms folded over chests. Alma and her sister quickly grabbed their food and ushered their families back into their cars. "Alicia was so upset she couldn't stop crying," Alma recounted. "None of us wanted to eat after that. It was very scary. We were afraid they were going to follow us out to our cars or start something with Alejandro."

Alma switched to a day shift as of that summer, and Alejandro, Sr. quit his second job. To their credit, I felt, they did this to spend more time with their children.

"My husband says that finally we can all eat supper together. He said he used to feel like *un perro abandonado* [a stray dog] because I always left food for him while I was away at work. Alejandro, Jr. ate more than I've seen him eat in a long time last night. I said to him, 'You must have been really hungry.' He said no; it was just that it felt so good to have his mother home cooking for him and serving the dinner that he didn't want it to end," Alma laughed. "I don't feel right. I think it's because I worked nights for so many years and my system isn't used to this change. But I know I did what was right for my family. My friends at work say they miss me. My two sisters I work with cried. They say it's not as good without me there. I always talked a lot and kind of fooled around, you know. It made the time go faster. They're begging me to come back. But I won't. I'm sorry, but my family needs me. I have to think of them first."

A lot happened for Alejandro that year, his last at an elementary school where he felt safe. He was "discovered" by girls and enjoyed that attention. He faced the reality of a public high school education and lowered his goals in terms of his choices of professions. He found that in the old "hood" and the new one, his color, Latino features, and accent are liabilities in the eyes of the "law." And for the first time in several years his family spent evenings together, in large part due to their concern for him.

Lately, Alejandro was more successful at "breaking the code" and orally reads noticeably better, yet he still battles with severe comprehension difficulties. He learned how to retreat into a world of popular music, phone calls from friends, and the household cleaning duties he has always excelled at. His borders as an adolescent Mexican-American became more dangerous as he faced the very real menaces of gangs, neighborhood violence, and blatant discrimination. The wall of his academic and economic difficulties impinged upon his hopes and dreams. He didn't quite know what he wanted to do, so frequently he did nothing. Yet, most of the time, he was a pleasure to be with—a sincere, kind young man.

He has come to trust a friend outside the family, who pushes him to read, to write, to think, to express his feelings. Someone who has no right to have examined his world but someone he and his family have graciously permitted to do so. Someone who has tried to tell his story. Although the notes, recordings, and interviews will now end, the friendship and concern will not. I have found, in particular, a strong, sweet friend in Alma.

Paths have crossed; connections were forged. I have told only part of the borders and dreams of a strong young man; and I have learned much more than I could ever return. And Alma, so central to this narrative, Alma has asked me to teach her, to work with her "the way you do for my son."

"I've thought of asking you for a while now. Maybe I could learn some English and to read a little. Maybe then I could help the kids more. I might not be able to do it but I just wonder, Christina." I wonder too.

Epilogue

We tell ourselves stories, in order to live.
—"On the Morning After the Sixties," J. Didion

About 6 months passed since Alejandro crossed the threshold into the hallowed halls of Crown High (a week later than expected due to a teachers' strike) and into the ranks of the thousands who carry the title of students in Chicago public high schools. Falling into this category, he bore burdens most of his more affluent counterparts will never face.

Cuts in staff experienced in the Chicago system in the fall caused him to lose the program he was promised in the spring. The budget deficit had to be lessened, we heard on all the T.V. news stations. Once just a curious announcement on the nightly news to me, I now realize in very specific human terms what these proposed cuts and changes can do to an average Chicago student. So, in Alejandro's case, over-burdened teachers at Crown shuffled students around less than 2 short weeks after their initial strike ended to spread their numbers more evenly.

"Chris, can you do something? They took me outta my classes and put me into ones I don't understand. I was doin' good in math and now I don't get anything they're doin'." The week before Alejandro had received the first A he had seen in years in his math class at Crown. Then he was switched to an upper level class that was not as full as his original one and he felt totally lost.

"I don't understand what happened, Alejandro," I said. "I'll call Sara and find out what's going on. You were so happy with your classes." The next day I contacted the guidance counselor who had helped set up Alejandro's program.

"They're not accepting the testing done at the college so he can't have the L.D. help," she told me.

"This is crazy!" I said. "They made his acceptance to Crown contingent upon doing that testing over the summer, and both the prin-

126

cipal and the technical program director said there would be no problem with the outside testing. You yourself told me that it would save almost a year of waiting for testing and placement by the Board to do it this way!"

"I know, I know. I don't know what happened but I'm going to get his program back for him first thing tomorrow morning. I know he can't handle that math class they gave him. They're just all so overburdened that no teacher wants a kid in a class if they absolutely don't have to have 'em. I'm doing the work of two other counselors that we lost myself. I've never seen it so bad before."

Alejandro called a couple of days later relieved that he had been given most of his program back, particularly his math class. I thought the crisis was over, and Sara and I talked about pushing for his outside testing to be reconsidered.

Within a couple of weeks, I received another distraught call from Alejandro and Alma.

"Chris, now they switched me to classes all in Spanish. I don't know enough Spanish to understand everything. I don't know how to write it at all. They said I gotta be in them though, but I don't want to," Alejandro recounted the latest program change.

"Chris, you know how my husband feels. We've never had him in Spanish classes," Alma took the phone. "He's so confused now, he's never been in the bilingual program and he liked his other classes."

"Alma, I don't understand it. I don't think they can make these big program changes without notifying you, especially into bilingual education. I'll call Sara again; this is just so frustrating. If they would just do what they promised both of us, things would be fine." Although I believed that a good bilingual program would have helped Alejandro immeasurably years ago, I felt sure that switching him to one in his freshman year was not the answer to his problems.

This time Sara told me that the director of Crown's bilingual program had just gotten around to checking her courses and saw that Alejandro was in ESL II, the level we agreed on last spring with his program director, Mr. Waters.

"She [the director] said that to be in ESL you have to be in the native language core courses," Sara told me. "I informed her that he came from a private school and had been taught all in English and had some ESL but needed more. She insisted that he had to be in Spanish classes to get ESL. 'You know, he can't have his cake and eat it too,' she told me, Chris." Her words burned in my mind. It seemed that an appropriate placement was something a student just didn't deserve in this system. On top of this development, I received a call from a Board of Education school psychologist saying that it was illegal to accept the college testing but that if we could add an IQ test by a licensed school psychologist and have the report co-signed by such a person, they could accept it. Master degree level L.D. specialists' testing such as that done at the university could be accepted only if done under the review of a licensed school psychologist, Dr. Whim told me.

"Okay," I thought. "I know a licensed school psychologist who consults at the college. I'll have the extra test done immediately and at least we can hold on to the L.D. help."

The extra testing was done within 2 days, but I worried what Alejandro's low scores would mean to the Crown psychologist, who did not seem sympathetic to the complexities involved in fair and un-biased test instruments for ESL kids. I now initiated calls outside of Crown High and contacted the director of bilingual education for the whole city. I described Alejandro's bilingual plight and she told me that if his parents requested ESL, Alejandro certainly had the right to attend it even if he was not enrolled in native language courses. I also told her about the testing he had received at the university to speed up procuring the help he needed and the new problems with this. She took the pertinent information and promised to rectify the ESL situation. Another fire doused. She added that concerning the evaluation, Alejandro had the right to have a bilingual psychologist review his testing.

"But this psychologist told me, when I asked her about the help of a bilingual psychologist to do the extra test she wanted, that it would take close to a year to get one."

"Oh, the psychologists will just tell you that to scare you into letting a monolingual psychologist take care of the case. Alejandro has the right to that help within 30 days," the director of bilingual education told me.

More promises were made to clear up everything as I reassured her of the good quality of the report in question and its recommendations.

Alejandro was, once again, put back into his original classes. In one month, his program had been changed half a dozen times. I wondered what happens to all the other Alejandros who have no advocate to undo the bureaucratic fumblings of the Board, those with no "*Maestra* Christina" to turn to. No wonder dropout figures among Latino students are so high, I thought. This system is incredibly insensitive and frustrating, and I speak English and have an advanced degree behind me. Imagine how overwhelmed the Almas of the city feel in trying to contend with it.

More brush fires would crop up soon. A slightly irate letter of retraction from the Board psychologist appeared in my mailbox, reports from Sara that all the directors' feathers were ruffled. Yet still, the college testing was not officially accepted and the only reason Alejandro was getting L.D. help (actually, illegally, I was reminded) was because of a certain pesky advocate's intercession.

Alejandro was happy once again, joined the soccer team, avoided the gangs that surround him, liked his teachers (except for one who taught ethnic history and reprimanded him for speaking Spanish to a friend), and had a girlfriend. I knew the curriculum had been "watered down," but it seemed to work for Alejandro. He loved his classes, made friends, and seemed to have found a group of soccer teammates who were not involved in the pervasive gang culture of Crown High. His program stabilized, at least for the moment.

In January, my family and I took a vacation to Florida for several days. Before our return flight we made a special stop at some souvenir shops to purchase gifts for the Juarez kids. We had candies and small Disney toys carefully packed at the top of our carry on bags to deliver to Alicia, Ricardo, Lupita, Almita, and Alejandro. Once home, my daughters turned on our answering machine. The first message was from Sara of Crown High. Call her right away, it said. Alejandro had been "jumped" by more than 20 African-American kids at his bus stop that day. He hadn't been taken to the hospital; she was worried.

I called Alma all evening but got busy signals every time. Early the next morning I finally got through and Alma recounted her son's ordeal of 3 days earlier.

"He got off the bus around Kedzie, right by the Jewel, and saw a bunch of African-American kids, Chris. A girl asked him and the other Latinos from the bus which gang they belonged to. They told her 'None.' But she didn't believe them. The other three boys realized something was wrong and started to run. Two got away but a big group of the kids started to punch Alejandro and his friend. His friend finally pulled away too and ran to a train station and got somebody to call the police." Alma was calm as she explained things to me. Yet it was a calmness born of irrevocability—the worst had happened.

I learned that before the police ever got involved, more than 20 kids circled Alejandro and beat him mercilessly. They pummeled his handsome face with their fists and kicked his chest and back over and over. They knocked his limp body into the gutter. All of this was taking place in broad daylight, Wednesday afternoon at about 3 p.m. as the traffic drove by. Two Mexican women on their way to an exercise class saw what happened and yanked Alejandro out of the gutter and into the back seat of their car. He managed to give them his address and they drove him to his house. His sister, Alicia, was home with the younger kids waiting for Alejandro, who was usually back by then. She was horrified when she saw her brother with his face all swollen and bleeding.

When Alma and her husband got home from work about half an hour later, Alicia met them on the front porch, crying hysterically that Alejandro had been hurt.

"I didn't know what to do, Chris. I was so scared. He was bleeding from his nose and mouth. His face was purple and all puffed up. I should have taken him to the hospital but I was too afraid," Alma explained. "I started to put ice on his face and I sent my husband to the police station. They had caught about a dozen of the kids and kept two of them at the police station. That's what I thought I should do first. They arrested those two. The other boy's parents, the one who got hit but got away and called the police, were there too. The Mexican kids identified the two held by the police. Now they're going to set up a court date. I don't know if it was the right thing to do. Now I worry that these kids they arrested will be looking for Alejandro."

"They weren't even from Crown," I heard Alejandro insist in the background. "I'm going to stay at Crown; it's my school and I like it there."

Alma continued, "I don't know, Chris. My husband and I are thinking about sending him to Mexico to stay with his grandfather to finish school. We're so close as a family and it's hard to even imagine being apart from him but we are so afraid. The police said we should have taken Alejandro to the hospital to have proof of how badly they beat him but I didn't know what to do. I was afraid. They asked us if we took pictures, but I never thought of that either."

I imagined how terrified Alma must have been. I completely understood her almost instinctual recourse to her homeland as refuge and safe harbor for her child. I had seen it happen with Mexican families I knew before. When confronted with even rumors of street violence, I had seen friends pack up their children, sending them to grandparents and aunts for the 4 years they feared most, high school in urban America.

"Sara called me," I said. "She left a message that you needed to take Alejandro to the hospital or to a doctor because his nose might be broken."

"I did finally take him, Chris. I should have taken him sooner but he didn't want to go. He was afraid too. But I did take him 2 days after it all happened. The doctor said it was close but that his nose wasn't broken."

At this point I began to cry, something Alma had never seen me do. Although we were on the phone, she realized.

"Oh, Chris, he's okay now, really." I could hear her gasp sympathetically as she recognized how terrible I felt. "You know, my husband and I just thank God those kids didn't have weapons. It could have been worse, really. He's sore but he's okay. Thank God. Now he'll be smarter too. He'll know that if he sees a group of kids like that he should stay on the bus till the next stop. He was just so innocent; he didn't know what to do. Now he knows. He's going to take a different bus route and I'm trying to see if my brother can give him a ride. We can't; we have to be in work at 6. His girlfriend's mother said they could help too. I just have to make plans."

Alma had woven another story for me, I realized—the story of her son's beating. She was deftly sewing and smoothing it into the fabric of her family's history, thanking God it wasn't worse, matching the seams of yet another urban injustice she had to accept.

"Oh, Alma, this is just what I was afraid of. It's terrible," I continued to cry. "I hate to say it but maybe you *should* send him to Mexico."

We talked some more about our fears of retaliation.

"The teachers at Crown met with Alejandro on Friday," said Alma. "They told him that now that this has happened, he absolutely cannot leave campus at any time during the school day and that he has to be really careful to go straight home, always. He cannot even leave to eat lunch with his friends."

Alejandro had befriended a group of boys from the soccer team. Sara Puente told me they were some of the nicest kids in the school and weren't gangbangers. Alejandro's joy was to go off campus with them to a pizza place frequented by the Mexican Crown students for lunch. At Crown, the surrounding restaurants and fast food chains' clientele were specifically defined by ethnicity. The Polish kids ate at the bowling alley snack bar, the African Americans controlled Dunkin' Donuts, the Mexicans had this pizza parlor. Crossing borders into the wrong source for food could be and had been fatal. Sara had told me just a few months earlier that it was in the shops that surrounded Crown that violence took place. "That's where one student was murdered last year, in the hamburger joint kitty corner from the school building. We can't control what happens there."

I don't believe Alejandro ever accepted that danger. After being on a closed campus for all of his elementary schooling, to be allowed to eat out was sheer pleasure for him and he felt safe within his group.

But now he brings lunch and eats alone because he was attacked. He waits in the library each day for his friends to return from lunch. Although Alma and I feel it is safer, it seems unfair that he, in effect, is punished because of his vulnerability.

"You know, Chris," Alma told me the afternoon I visited Alejandro to see for myself how he was faring, "we always taught our kids not to be prejudiced against African Americans. My brothers aren't like that. They don't agree. They say things to their kids about their ideas on the blacks. But we always told our kids it was wrong to be prejudiced. But you know, last week our car was stolen at work by some black men. Co-workers saw them but couldn't stop it. They destroyed most of it. In that −25 degree weather we had to take two buses to work at 6 a.m. while our car's being fixed. Now this happens to our son a couple of weeks later. It's hard not to say something. It breaks my heart to hear Alejandro tell me that when he sees a group of black kids at school his stomach just gets gripped with fear. I don't want him to feel that way. Even though all this has happened, I still don't want him to feel that way."

Alma and her husband, once again, are models for me of incredibly thoughtful, ethical people for whom the concepts of equality, nonviolence, and justice have concrete referents in their everyday struggle to survive. I am touched deeply by their staunch values.

To the school's credit, Alejandro appreciated his treatment by most of his teachers at Crown. He was adamant that he could figure out a way to get to and from school safely and that he will remain at Crown. For the first time in his educational journey he is seen as the "good boy" he always strove to be recognized as. Despite his rough voyage over the waters of bureaucratic categories and labels, they seem to have noticed at Crown that this young man breaks the mold, defies the image of the "bad" minority kid who underachieves in school. Although not a model student, although not preoccupied with academic shortcomings, he persisted in moving along, fulfilling requirements, being cooperative, upbeat, and decent—the "good boy" his parents have taught him to be. Yet his daily trip to and from school, an uneventful journey I and many parents take for granted for our children, was filled with anxiety for him and his parents. He scaled these borders with quiet determination. And now, those incredibly high statistics on the Latino dropout rates in major cities make perfect sense to me, and like the factual T.V. announcement of budget cuts for schools, they have been brought to life for me in the person of Alejandro.

Postscript

As I revised and edited Alejandro's story a little over a year after the bus stop episode, Alma called late one Sunday night, as she used to when I had been working with Alejandro. It was good to hear the familiar string of greetings to me and my whole family, yet I sensed that this was more than a friendly call. The rides to and from school that Mr. and Mrs. Juarez had finally been able to set up for Alejandro had fallen through. The classmate who picked him up, and whom I had met a few weeks earlier when visiting the Juarezes, had been suspended from school. Alma and her husband were worried, for when they resumed dropping Alejandro off at the bus stop, it looked to them like a very rough crowd of fellow commuters.

"Chris, he seems to be hanging around with more and more guys from school. We don't like it. And, well, we didn't want to tell you when you came to visit last time, *porque nos da vergüenza* [because we are ashamed] *y él también tiene vergüenza* [and Alejandro is also ashamed], but Alejandro has been doing very badly at school for a while now. Chris, I've been thinking about this for a long time and it just doesn't make sense to me to keep sending him to school when he refuses to read or write at home and never does homework any more. The teachers at Crown offered to have him stay after school for help each day and my husband says he'll pick him up right at school afterward, but Alejandro doesn't want to stay. We're very frustrated and very, very sad. My husband is sick about it. But we think that at least if he goes to work instead of school, he'll be away from those tough kids. I know they're *gangeros* [gang members]. You know, he's failed so many courses, he won't pass his second year and he's 16 now. What do you think, Chris?" Alma waited.

I never anticipated having to answer that question; she was looking for my consent to having Alejandro drop out of school. No, I
thought, this isn't happening—but it was.

"What about going to school in Mexico?" I rebounded. "You were
thinking of sending him to relatives in Tu Patarrillo." I, too, was willing to run back to the arms of the motherland I had grown to love and
trust through Alma's stories.

"Well, Chris, when we went back there at Christmas, I saw some
things that worried me. The boys in my town are drinking a lot, even
12-year-olds. A lot of young girls were pregnant on *El Rancho* [the
ranch]. I'm afraid Alejandro would get involved with that and it would
be too hard on my father to handle him."

"Oh, Alma, I'm so sad," I sighed. "What kinds of grades is Alejandro getting at Crown?" I asked.

"Oh, Chris, a lot of Fs. A lot. He's never wanted us to tell you.
I'm always asking him to go to his room and read or practice math.
You know, he has the most trouble with his math class. But he doesn't.
He just talks on the phone. Every day that we leave him at the bus stop
I worry more. Every time I get called to the phone at work my chest
pounds and I immediately think it's Alejandro; he's been hurt at school
again, he's in trouble with the gangs. It scares me so much. I'm always
anticipating a call like that."

She continued, "You know, Chris, I told Alejandro that we would
make the sacrifice and somehow get the money together for him to go
to a Catholic high school. I've done without things for myself before.
I can do it again. But I don't even know where to look for a school like
that."

"Alma, I don't think any Catholic high school would accept him
with almost all Fs from Crown. And they probably wouldn't have the
kind of classes and help he'd need. I've heard of one Catholic vocational high school but it's not near your home and I just don't think
they'd accept him anyway."

"I understand," she said softly. "That's what I thought. You know,
we have a nephew that dropped out and went to work for 2 years, then
he went back to school and really worked hard to get his GED. My
husband and I were thinking that maybe Alejandro would do the same.
Maybe he'd realize how hard he'll have to work, at the worst jobs,
without a diploma. My nephew is doing well now; he's been promoted
at the factory. I just don't know what to do, Chris, but I *am* sure that
I don't like him around the kids I see by his school."

"Well, Alma," I began, "I've always said to you that his safety comes
first. We just can't ignore that. If he's failing everything at school and

won't go for help or do his homework, I can see your point. Why keep sending him and putting him into contact with the group you've worried about. I feel terrible saying that, but maybe you should let him leave school and go to work. But I don't think he'll be able to handle taking the GED test. His reading's not strong enough. I wonder if any work programs exist where he can get training without a diploma. I'll have to look into that."

Periodically I could hear Alejandro in the background vainly attempting excuses or debating his use of the telephone. I could envision him seated at the heavy dark wood kitchen table that supported him as strongly as his parents did, looking sheepish, floating through this crisis as he had done through others before.

"Sometimes, Christina," Alma added, "sometimes I honestly think he acts like a 5- or 6-year-old. I look at Alicia and how hard she works. I know she'll succeed at school. She gets mad at Alejandro. My sister took Alicia, Almita, and Lupita to the circus today and when they got home, Alejandro was lying on the couch with the phone and Alicia got really mad at him. There were things scattered around, and Alicia told him that there was no reason for the house to look a mess and that he shouldn't just be lying around. She doesn't have patience with him."

"Oh I know Alicia will do well, Alma. She'll be able to find a scholarship easily and she'll be the one to make your and your husband's dream of a good education and a career come true. Ricardo too; he doesn't have problems learning."

"I know, oh, yes, Chris, I know. From the time he was very little I could see a difference from Alejandro and my other children in his memory and his speech. I just worry that if we give permission for Alejandro to quit school that it will set a bad example for Ricardo, Almita, and Lupita too. I don't worry about Alicia; she's so serious and conscientious that I know it won't affect her. But I worry about the little ones. You know, Chris, you really helped me to understand that Alejandro truly has problems with learning. Before we knew you, my husband and I just kept thinking that he didn't try hard enough. At least we know now that there was something else going on. That really helped us face all of this."

"Oh, yes, Alma, he really does have problems in reading and writing. He's still confused between English and Spanish and he really has memory problems. You know, I never expected him to get As or Bs at Crown. But with special courses and the help there I thought he could pass with Cs. I know it's hard for him; I knew that all along." I was almost thinking out loud by then.

"Christina, do you know how old he has to be to be allowed to, to leave school?" Alma asked hesitantly.

This was really happening. Alma wanted the particulars; she was tapping her source for school information: me. She had made her decision and I could not refute it. Part of me felt that I should and I knew that I might be able to persuade her and Alejandro to insist on their son staying in school. But she had thought it all through with the pragmatic reasoning I had so often seen her excel at. She was doing what was best for her child's safety and she knew that. It seemed almost instinctual, like a mother in the wild protecting her young.

"Gee, Alma, I'll ask my husband. I don't even know how that all works," I said mechanically. I could hardly bear to tell her, to assist her, yet I knew that I should. It was strangely analogous to helping someone make funeral arrangements or get things ready for an inevitable loss. The loss of a dream, I thought. The palpable aching loss of a parent's dream.

"Sixteen, with the parent's permission," I heard my husband, who was at one time a high school guidance counselor, answer. And I relayed the information woodenly. Alma related more of her well-thought-out plans. Alejandro would start to work with his cousin in a candy factory. She and her husband would drive him to and from work. . . . One hundred thirty a week, full time. . . . Alma had done her homework.

"That's less than minimum wage," my husband commented. "What a shame."

"Maybe if I spent more time helping Alejandro and less time writing his story this wouldn't have happened," I found myself saying. Yet deep in my heart I knew that I had always felt that I was merely plugging the proverbial hole in the dike and that the threat of flood was never really under control. How could I finish his story, I wondered, drenched in my latest Sunday night phone call from Alejandro's home.

Without even verbalizing it, I knew what I would do. I would write about what happened; I had to write about what happened. Alejandro was not going to have a happy ending; the after-school special storyline—where the inner city kid makes it through education and hard work—was not going to be his. Alejandro gave up. Alejandro Juarez, Jr. was going to become part of the chilling statistics on the Latino dropout rate in Chicago of which I wrote over a year ago as I mapped out my doctoral work. The wall Langston Hughes described had succeeded in hiding the light of his dream. Naively, perhaps, *I* never dreamed it would happen. Not my Alejandro. Not Alma's son. He always kept plugging away, like the Ever-Ready rabbit, he just kept on marching. That was my perception. Or perhaps my deception.

His young religion teacher at Sorrowful Mother was more percep-
tive than I was. She worried that he would succumb to peer pressure
in high school. And he did. His school friends offered him fun, rides,
"laughs," as I heard him say. They encouraged him to find a job, dis-
couraged him from schoolwork, and he readily followed.

Mrs. Lago said that Alejandro gave up on himself in her class and
now he gave up, in effect, on all of school. I found myself saying to
Alma, "You know, as much as I disagreed with some things Sister
Eleanor did, at least Alejandro studied there, he managed to pass."
Inside I wondered if what I described as heavy-handed discipline was a
viable alternative but could not readily embrace that idea. "Yes, Chris,
I've thought of that. So has my husband. I've even thought about sending him to one of those very strict schools where they live there and
have regulations all set up. But I don't know if there are any he could
attend."

"Probably not, Alma. Private boarding schools are expensive and
would want high grades for admission. Other schools with that setup
would be, well, like reform schools for kids who've been in trouble with
the law and I know you don't want that."

"Oh, no, Chris. But you know, Alejandro did okay when we let
him work part time at the pizza place before Christmas. He never missed
a day and he learned his job well. He always gave me his paycheck, too.
He wanted to help out with food bills; I remember he wanted to buy
me a new dress. My husband says maybe, with the extra money Alejandro could bring in, we could save enough to move to the suburbs
and get away from the gangs, find better schools. Alejandro has always
been very good about helping to support the family."

There it was again. Alma could always resurrect hope, even at times
of the most bitter disappointment. Her son might not graduate now,
perhaps never, but in her eyes he was, at heart, still a good boy.

As I had promised Alma, I asked a good friend of mine, who had
guided me through much of my dissertation, if he knew of any work
training programs for Alejandro. Although he did not know of any, he
promised to look into it for me. I told him that I had to write this last
part of the story of Alejandro and he agreed. "This isn't the end," he
said, empathically, with his own indefatigable hope for children. This
can't be the end, I hoped. If I had learned anything during this past
year-and-a-half, it was not to permit despair. I had learned that from
Alma, who became the soul of the stories I penned, for they were her
stories. With her inimitable resilience, she reminded me of her faith in
her son, her love for him despite his failings. Although her dreams had
dimmed, she still had hope.

I began this story recalling images from Steinbeck's novel *The Pearl*. I could not help but see the parallels once again as Alma and her husband relinquished their hope in an education, that elusive pearl, for their son. "Let us bury it and forget the place. Let us throw it back into the sea" (Steinbeck, 1947, p. 54), Juana says of their pearl at the end of that story. Something in Alma's voice echoes in Juana's decision.

The image of Steinbeck's character Lennie in the book *Of Mice and Men* surfaced as well. I found myself re-reading the last scene of the book. "And Lennie answered her, 'I tried, Aunt Clara, ma'am. I tried and tried. I couldn't help it'" (Steinbeck, 1937, p. 205). Lennie waits for his buddy George, knowing that he has unintentionally done something very wrong. He imagines conversations in which he is being ridiculed and chastised for his failings; he cannot imagine what is about to befall him. It was the only novel, indeed the only written language, that I had ever seen Alejandro connect with and be touched by in school. I had patterned my title of Alejandro's story after it. I realized, painfully, that, like Lennie, Alejandro *had* tried, he had tried and tried for years. He too, in many ways, just couldn't help it.

Perhaps Alejandro will keep plugging away, but in a different arena, toward a path not yet clear to me or to his family. The church bell in my town is now tolling on a sunny spring afternoon. When I first ended this collection of narratives, it was snowy and stormy as dusk settled over the meandering river outside the aging library where I write. Now I look at that river flowing calmly, yet resolutely, toward an end I cannot see. The sun is in my eyes, and I can't help but think that, like Alma's spirit, it is fighting the advent of evening. I will end these narratives before it sets.

May the telling of Alejandro's story in some small way smooth borders for other students. May it encourage dreams too stubborn to fade completely even while, of necessity, they must be adjusted drastically. May Alejandro and others like him learn to cope with the obstacles that make meaningful and safe education an impossible dream rather than a basic right. May the educational community find ways to improve conditions and the courage to do so.

Educational Implications: Beyond Borders

Narrative imitates life, life imitates narrative.
—*Life as Narrative*, J. Bruner

Olson (1990) wrote that narratives "provide a format into which experienced events can be cast in an attempt to make them comprehensible, memorable, shareable" (pp. 100–101). The Juarez family's experiences that I chronicled certainly support Olson's statement. Once "cast," they formed a powerful story.

The narratives told here also provide fertile ground in which educational implications flourish. A garden of potential connections between the Juarezes' experiences and the world of education begs cultivation. Educators seeking to open borders that prohibit and curtail academic success for students who struggle with lived experiences similar to Alejandro's may find in his story the seeds of curricular innovation, programmatic considerations, and administrative alternatives. More essentially, I believe the Juarez narratives offer concrete, poignant examples of what educational jargon often fails to reveal in compassionate and comprehensible terms. Skills-based reading instruction, whole language, second language acquisition, immersion English programs, hands-on learning, culturally relevant literature, learning disabilities, and a dozen other instructional labels and phrases literally come to life through Alejandro's struggles. His experiences and those of his parents become the very understandable media through which a picture of urban education emerges. Like a representational, realistic style of art, they create an image that is easy to interpret and comprehend.

In as straightforward and unpretentious manner as a pencil sketch, and with the innocence of a child's crayon drawing, Alma's stories somehow capture perfectly and with ease the complex and multifaceted problem of education for diverse students in this country. When

139

she asks, "Maestra, what is art?" in trying to choose enrichment classes for her son, or when she struggles to comprehend the psychoeducational jargon of a multidisciplinary staffing for her daughter, it serves as a lens through which educators may focus on a kind of parent they need to see and appreciate more clearly. When Alejandro has no word or meaning for swan in any language, yet is expected to comprehend a story where that knowledge is crucial, or must write a description of a trip he has never made to a dentist's office, the concept of background experiences and schema theory is highlighted with clarity, its importance heightened. When school notes cannot be read in English or Spanish and it results in just one boy wearing a school uniform as punishment on a field trip, when parents are prisoners of a fearful respect for educators, and cannot decipher the oral language needed to participate in a school graduation program, communication needs between the home and school are poignantly dramatized. When a skills-driven curriculum saps meaning from literacy for a child who then ignores print in his environment, avoids books, and retreats into music, movies, and peer lore for information and stimulation, the theoretical battle between whole language and skills-based instruction clearly portrays the counterproductive potential of exclusive curricular policies.

As I look back on my time with Alejandro and his family, I realize that the metaphor of journey is a strong and persistent one for me. We shared as well as struggled through new experiences, learned from and about each other in ways that can happen only when people are "on the road" together. Eighth grade was our pathway, Chicago our setting. There is an intensity to the time spent with fellow travelers, a feeling that one must see and do all that one can before the trip ends. I always felt that Alejandro and I had miles and miles to go before he left the shelter of his elementary school. A commitment also exists to explore the novel, to sample new surroundings, to risk change and challenges. Alejandro sampled something new with Sister Faith, but in many ways it was too late for him to enjoy a change. Although I follow a basic route and itinerary when I travel, or teach, it is never set in stone and there is always room for unexpected detours into new horizons. Individually tutoring Alejandro became the main street of our journey, and his mother's stories, recollections, and concerns the vehicle for the many side trips we experienced. Recalling the borders and dreams I encountered with the Juarezes, certain areas of impact on Alejandro's education emerge strongly on the map of our course. Like the most memorable events in traveling, they arise again and again in the stories I tell of the trip to friends who could not share the journey. Alejandro consistently bumped into several cultural borders that always presented him with problems. Differences between his home and school cultures, a "culture" of low textual literacy, and a peer culture that devalued academic achievement thwarted his educational success significantly. In reflecting on pedagogical changes for him, their impact cannot be overlooked.

In an anthropological and ethnographic sense, Alejandro experienced incongruities between his home and school cultures. As other cross-cultural researchers discovered (Au, 1980; Au & Kawakami, 1991; Au & Mason, 1983; Emerson, 1983; Gibson, 1987; Heath, 1982, 1983, 1986; Phillips, 1983), Alejandro's ways of learning and familial values differed from those esteemed by traditional educators. Learning through observation, supportive gradual mastery of skills, cooperation in tasks, collaboration in negotiating life's everyday trials were emphasized by a large family accustomed to working together. Yet in school, tasks were assigned with little emphasis on modeling, individual achievement was prized, collaboration for support was seen negatively as cheating. School skills seemed distinct from and unrelated to real life. Literacy, in particular, was not woven into the fabric of his family's environment, although it enjoyed a wider definition—a "literacy" of experiences and rich oral history. It might have provided a link between his home and the world of education. Instead, school skills remained completely disjointed from authentic tasks, indeed, disjointed from each other. Researchers King and Rentel (1981) wrote of their observation that in schools serving predominantly economic, social, or linguistic minorities, the curriculum often is reorganized into a more segmented, subdivided, and decontextualized approach called skill-building. The assumption appears to be that educators must be able to break down "skills" into small, comprehensible subcomponents for children who do not bring the desired middle-class language and learning styles to school. Some researchers (Farr & Daniels, 1986) believe that, particularly in literacy learning, even mainstream students do not engage in enough extended and interrelated experiences in schools. Skill-building certainly was the philosophy of Sorrowful Mother School. The further Alejandro fell behind in literacy activities, the more skill-building he was fed, with the best of intentions. Meanwhile, the whole language revolution was taking place in the field of reading and also was being recommended for bilingual students. Educational researchers in second language acquisition were writing of how crucial it was to have bilingual students "be engaged with whole, authentic written discourse" (Edelsky, 1986, p. 95). Others wrote of their concern that a holistic approach to literacy was critical for students from nonmainstream homes "where writing is not a central part of parents' occupations or of family affairs, and where the rates of parental illiteracy are high" (Farr & Daniels, 1986, p. 63). Yet, Alejandro experienced a curriculum that aligned itself clearly, by administrative decision, in one methodological camp versus another—skill-building versus whole language. The result of this methodological position was, I believe, disastrous for Alejandro. Not only did he deal with cultural incongruencies between home and school in an anthropological sense, but he also dealt with a particular school culture that did not match his academic needs. I am not espousing total allegiance to the whole language philosophy to the exclusion of skills teaching, but am instead suggesting that elements of both philosophies could have been melded to create a meaningful curriculum for a student such as Alejandro. A holistic, integrated approach to education might have offered Alejandro a chance to make connections his parents could not facilitate for him. Due to their struggle with textual literacy, the two worlds of home and school were even further separated for Alejandro. If ever a student needed a holistic approach to literacy and learning in general, to hands-on experiences with concrete materials, to relevant literature strong in story and rich in context, it was Alejandro Juarez, Jr.

In trying to piece together the puzzle of his academic failure, I began to gain a deeper understanding of the tangible impact approaches to learning and methodologies of teaching could have on a student. The window I had into his everyday home life brought to life such educational concepts as integrated learning and performance-based outcomes—both of which deal with connected and realistic approaches to learning. I remembered, for example, that in the area of math Alejandro was diagnosed as being particularly weak in fractions and I recognized an emblematic instance in his home life that illuminated for me the kind of bridges he did not have between school skills and authentic tasks. His mother and sister wanted to make an "American" cake from a packaged mix for Mr. Juarez, who enjoyed cake he had eaten that my daughter baked. Despite basically being able to read the recipe from the box, Alicia and Alma could not comprehend exactly how to go about baking the Pillsbury chocolate cake mix they purchased. Their unfamiliarity with dry and liquid measurement—cups and fractions of cups, measuring cups and spoons—made the steps in the recipe incomprehensible for them. Alma cooked as her mother and older sisters taught her to cook, on a ranch in the heart of rural Mexico. The familiar red labeled, clear glass measuring cups and set of nested measuring spoons common to my kitchen and many mainstream children's were not part of life in Juan de Carreo. Activities such as cutting fruit in halves and quarters and calling kids' attention to those labels, which

I and my peers did routinely when our children were younger, were not routine in the Juarez household. I had been present on many occasions when Alma prepared food for her family and mine. During those times, cooking seemed to be regarded as a gender-specific task in which female children took part in marginal, authentic tasks, such as fetching ingredients. Alma cooked and her daughters quietly and attentively observed. It was not perceived as a time for integrating school skills, practice in counting, "experiencing" fractions. It was no wonder to me why her oldest son had such difficulty with the concept of fractions, even as an adolescent. They had no concrete referents in his life, no practical application. He literally had no earthly reason for using them. Alma did not conceptualize her role as a parent as one that included academic skill-building. Although she would have been limited in recognizing such opportunities for school-oriented teaching due to her own limited schooling, I doubt that she would have assumed that role even in areas in which she could have been helpful, such as counting and managing money. Like many Mexican parents of young children I had met, Alma's sense of education for her offspring was much broader than the mainstream, suburban push for early academic achievement and school-related skills so common in my parenting experience. (For more background on what Mexican-American parents see as their responsibility in raising their children, see Valdés, 1996.) Alma and her peers often used the phrase *bien educado* [well educated] when describing goals for their children. In Spanish, the phrase connotes a wider sense of raising well-bred, mannerly, clean, educated, respectful, responsible, articulate, loved, and loving children rather than solely academically well-prepared ones. Children were taught to fulfill parents' and teachers' expectations obediently, yet each set of activities—parental and pedagogical—was viewed as separate from the other. Alma's desire for Alejandro to be *bien educado*, which she articulated repeatedly, was an amalgam of academic, social, cultural, and religious aspirations for him. I cannot help but recognize hers as a healthier, nobler goal than the emphasis on academic and athletic competition and achievement I have witnessed as a mainstream, middle-class parent. As she and her husband strive to raise respectful and competent children in a world that neither respects them nor acknowledges their strengths, her aspirations better address some of the most basic curricular questions: "What knowledge is most worthwhile? Why is it worthwhile? How is it acquired or created?" (Schubert, 1986, p. 1).

In addition to the multilayered cultural incongruities he faced in education, Alejandro stumbled through the potholes of what I term a culture of low and challenged textual literacy. Negotiating print was a consistent problem for his parents and extended family. Alma and her husband openly mourned and reproached themselves for not being able to overcome their failure—low textual literacy—for the sake of their children.

"As I see my children, one by one, having difficulties in school, I know it is because of me," Alma frequently told me. "I know I don't have a good memory. I see it in myself, at work and at home. So how can I get disappointed in Alejandro when he can't remember things at school? He gets it from me. And I can't help him; I can't help any of our children with homework, I can't help them with school." The challenge of low textual literacy had far-reaching effects in Mr. and Mrs. Juarez' daily lives and their children's; "no bedroom storyreading" (Heath, 1986) was not the only consequence it held.

There was little use of textual literacy in the Juarez household. It was a task relegated to school; it had to be. Information in their home was learned orally from family, work, or community networks. Learning occurred through observation, apprenticeship, or discovery through experience, all of which were rare forms of learning at Alejandro's school. His family's culture of low textual literacy continuously surfaced as a major obstacle to his academic success and to the economic security of the family. I stress their illiteracy's effect academically and economically because I firmly believe that there are other ways in which their struggle with the written word has benefitted the Juarez children. It has taught them resourcefulness and the advantages of cooperation and collaboration, and serves as a potent impetus to appreciate educational opportunities. It has, as well, united them firmly as a family, although at times they are united in fear.

Although intensely supportive of his education, Alejandro's parents are unaware of how to facilitate his school success. They are vague in their career expectations for their son, although they are clear and emphatic in their desire for him to pursue better employment situations than they have experienced. Delgado-Gaitan (1990), in her studies with Mexican and Mexican-American parents, found that what she labeled their folk theory of success (what they perceived success to mean in the U.S. context) was based on their perception of their own low status in this society and their desire to prevent their children from experiencing the oppression they had as immigrants. The parents Delgado-Gaitan interviewed recognized a need for their children to learn English, but the only other concrete advice they could give their children for school success was to obey their teachers. This is similar to the situation I observed in the Juarez household. Mrs. Juarez periodically asked me what I thought of Alejandro's English proficiency and often reminded me of how important both she and her husband felt it was for him to achieve fluency in his second language. They repeatedly recounted encouraging him to converse with native English speakers in their new neighborhood to develop his English abilities. They lectured him on behaving in school and listening to his teachers, even when they admitted doubts about teacher behaviors. His parents also recognized the importance of having access to books and encouraged him to go to the library, although both their own and Alejandro's reading problems and unfamiliarity with library practices greatly hindered what he could accomplish there on his own. Nieto (1992) in her textbook on multicultural education, wrote, "The fact remains . . . that European American, middle-class parents, given their own experiences and exposure to the schools, are much more aware of those activities that lead to academic success than are poor and working class parents from linguistic and cultural backgrounds different from the mainstream" (p. 185). I found that Alejandro's situation bore this statement out even more dramatically due to the textual illiteracy that further challenged his parents in actively guiding or assisting their son's academic pursuits.

The rich oral literacy and collaborative learning that abounded in the Juarez household seemed not to be tapped by his schooling; his educators seemed unaware of the connections between home and school that might have facilitated learning despite the literacy problem. Like Moll and Diaz's (1987) study, mine revealed that homework and communications from school were the main literacy events in the Juarez household. Yet both parents were locked out of participation in these literacy activities due to the problems they faced with written language. The Juarezes' ability to verbally interact with their children, ask genuine questions, delight in humorous stories, share time and ideas is completely overlooked by the school systems they encountered. Interviewing, storytelling, participation in hands-on activities, sharing expertise and "living knowledge" from the community (Moll, 1992, p. 232) all hold potential for families such as Alejandro's to begin to build bridges and cross difficult borders into their children's school lives. Although I believe that parental participation from culturally diverse families should not be made or expected to fit the mainstream mold, differing aspirations and philosophies should be respected and recognized. Such parents should, I feel, be given venues feasible for entry into the academic realm. Alma, by choice, focuses on a wider panorama in her definition of education for her children. A visit to an aunt who is ill, for example, to help with the care of cousins, is likely to supersede any design for parental input on a homework assignment, no matter how sensitive and innovative. To expect something different, perhaps, would be too culturally demanding. The involvement of diverse parents, illiterate parents, parents who for centuries have not had positive school-related experiences and images, presents a challenge for educators, yet is so crucial to reaching toward an education that is meaningful and humane. The assumption of deficiency on the part of minority parents calls for new understandings based on ethnographic research by teachers and administrators committed to excellence in education and able to recognize and focus on what is there rather than what is not.

Finally, although Alejandro's parents relentlessly try to shield him from the influence of his peer culture, he must contend with this influence at school and it noticeably affects his responses to education. My data clearly showed that Alejandro enjoys the dynamics of a familiar group of adolescents and quickly adopts the most visible and vocal attitudes, even if they impede his school success. In elementary school it was as if he needed to get all his desire for peer companionship satisfied during his school day, even if it adversely affected his academic achievement, because he knew he would rarely be permitted to associate with peers after school hours. With high school came much more dramatic peer influences as discipline greatly loosened. All of Alejandro's attention turned to the fun that boys and girls in his classes could offer, and his parents began to begrudgingly acquiesce to the constant pressure he put on them to be with his friends.

Among his social group, adolescent Mexican males, school success is not frequently an overriding concern. Although in Alejandro's private school experience high dropout rates were not as prevalent as they are in public high schools (Lee, 1985), that preselected private school experience has ended for him. He also is no longer part of a predominantly Mexican school population. For the first time in Alejandro's educational career he faces conflicts among peer subgroups, as his high school is quite evenly divided among African-Americans, Latinos, and Caucasian students of Eastern European descent. He confronts open and visible gang activities and affiliations, and the strong arm of Sister Eleanor no longer protects him from their influence.

In the United States, he experiences something akin to a battle zone just to reach his place of schooling. Non-Mexican peers refuse to believe that he has no gang affiliation, and the stops for the mass transit system, which he must use, become an urban battleground upon which he has been assaulted for not flashing gang colors. His peers of Mexican heritage encourage him to minimize schooling and find jobs that swallow large blocks of time for small salaries to be spent on new clothing, old cars, and popular music. When he attempts to gather with friends or cousins in the neighborhood to play basketball or baseball, they are automatically suspected of gang activity and confronted by local police officers and detectives. His grades are so dismally low that he is not permitted to be part of sanctioned athletic teams with schoolmates. As an alternative to involvement with peers, his parents offer unending chores around the house, or visits to relatives' homes as pastimes. His parents do not have the luxury of much leisure time in their own work-filled lives where overtime shifts are routine and necessary to stay afloat economically. They cannot understand why their son complains of being bored at home when they would welcome his help with the burden of household maintenance and would welcome his participation in their large extended family. They are not aware of, or do not feel comfortable with, youth programs through the YMCA, Latino groups like Casa Azatlan that offer academic help and leisure activities, or church-associated events. Or they fear the mass transportation needed for their children to participate in such programs. Consequently, the pastime their son chooses is to hang out with other students who also find schooling in their second language difficult and ignore a curriculum that holds no meaning for them. Girls his age pursue him, for he is considered very handsome and sweet. Some try to help him in school when they realize his pronounced difficulties there. Among Latino adolescent girls, school success is often valued. But they do not succeed in changing his academic performance, for his learning problems are serious, his own literacy minimal. The girls become one more distraction from school, as hours are spent in flirtation over the phone. He and his parents constantly argue about his friends; Alma and Alejandro, Sr. valiantly try to keep him from them but are beginning to fear that he will totally rebel if they do not acquiesce to allowing peer contact.

The solution to this final "culture" of impact on Alejandro's education seems the most overwhelming to me. It requires, I fear, the unrealistic goal of solving societally based problems in entire communities. Organized leisure activities are not well funded in cities; gangs are entrenched in urban life. All of these factors are entwined with his struggle to become educated and conspire against the realization of dreams for a better life. The Mexican parents I have seen who have overcome gang involvement or repercussions and negative peer influence have resorted to flight to the motherland during adolescence or have had wider connections in the community and have found other pastimes for their children. Through school, church, and family, something or someone has reached their sons and daughters, who usually have had more academic success and stronger literacy within their families than has Alejandro. The singular glimmer of hope I see in this area is that educators and administrators will realize the importance of quality after-school programs, linked to communities, fashioned to be inclusive and sensitive to diversity. Such opportunities truly are not luxuries or extras; I believe they are essential in today's cities.

Alejandro's story taught me that the need for responsiveness in education is pronounced and paramount. Broadened responses to cultural differences that go beyond the superficiality of foods and folkdances, to acknowledgment of diverse ways of learning, using language, doing, and valuing, are essential. Scaffolding learning, supporting it from an appropriate and relevant point, requires responsiveness to the cultural ground from which that learning can be built. Freire and Macedo (1987) suggest that educators "need to use their students' cultural universe as a point of departure" (p. 127) in the sense of a point from which students can take off educationally and soar—and grow in cultural pride rather than disdain for their own physical features. In addition, widened responses to parents who do not fit the mainstream, school-oriented mold yet offer new shapes in which to cast parental concern and participation, are sorely needed. Responsiveness to the possibility of a curriculum that goes beyond traditional academic borders and more fully connects the various landscapes of life—home, school, and community—seems critically indicated. To fashion such responses, "ongoing ethnography to inform teaching" (Moll & Diaz, 1987, p. 311) could become an invaluable tool in teaching rather than something reserved for anthropologists and researchers.

The acceptance of varied responses to learning, implementation of innovative evaluation methods in schooling, also seems crucial for students in Alejandro's situation. When allowed to draw in response to reading material, or to dramatize comprehension of a story, or even to verbally discuss reactions to a book, Alejandro met with success—a rare event in his schooling where paper and pencil tasks were the usual performance outcome. The willingness to broaden responses to children, to their styles of responding, seems essential to me as I reflect on the story I experienced. Au and Kawakami (1991) discuss in their research with Hawaiian children, their belief in a hybrid classroom culture where diverse children can become a community of learners, sharing relevant school experiences as teachers and students mutually adapt to each other's styles and values. If we adopt a multidimensional view of learning where cultural conformity need not be the price of academic success, I believe that, in the future, the stories that diverse children will tell us of their education will be more positive and successful.

I am acutely aware of the prudence of caution in generalizing not only from a single-subject case study, but also from narratives and the interpretive process they involve. Smith (1981) notes, "No narrative version can be independent of a particular teller and occasion of telling" (p. 215), and Carter (1993) writes, "We are, in the very act of story making . . . imposing structures and meaning on events" (p. 9). In my narratives of Alejandro's eighth-grade year and some key events that prefaced and followed it, I tried to present an accurate picture of the events I witnessed and of which I was told. I strove to include the positive and the negative I observed in his educational journey and to present the many contradictions I found in the months of interactions I watched. Yet, "what we tell and how we tell it is a revelation of what we believe" (Carter, 1993, p. 9). I am sure that my narratives reflect my belief in the child's right to a sensitive education and fair and just treatment, as well as my deep appreciation for the Mexican culture. Yet, case studies do not "preclude the careful framing of patterns with respect to certain themes" (Carter, 1993, p. 10), and the study of narratives "has now become a positive source of insight for all branches of human and natural science" (Mitchell, 1981, p. ix). I am heartened in particular by the support I felt for such research from Elliot Eisner (1988), who wrote that to use narrative data required courage, for "narratives are regarded as 'soft,' and soft data do not inspire confidence among the tough-minded . . . one needs to able to trust on the basis of coherence, utility and the often ineffable sense of rightness that true stories display" (p. ix). I so often felt that "sense of rightness" as I wrote my narratives, for they reflected so compellingly other stories I read of immigrant and minority struggles with life and education. They mirrored, too, the data presented by educational ethnographers studying the school success and failure of minority children in the United States. I felt that a natural process of triangulation and validation arose as I became a participant observer in Alejandro's life.

The educational implications that grew from the stories of Alejandro are almost endless. Those I recorded are only a fraction of what I recognized. As I draw these few connections to a close, I caution that the pedagogical suggestions I made, the doorways carved from ethnographic data, may hold true only for Alejandro Juarez, Jr. Yet, if in their presentation an educator recognizes the image of a student, however faint or partial, and feels that "sense of rightness" in the story I have told, perhaps, if nothing more, it will serve to encourage that teacher to listen (with heart) to another student's story and create connections between lives and schools of his or her own for that student's journey.

As educators, families, and communities, let us look for bridges to span borders and support dreams for all children, of all backgrounds.

Hay tantísimas fronteras
que dividen a la gente,
pero por cada frontera
existe también un puente.
(Gina Valdés, 1982, p. 2)

There are so many borders
that divide people,
but for each border
there also exists a bridge.
(Translated by Chris Carger, 1994)

References

Anzaldúa, G. (1987). *Borderlands/La Frontera: The new mestiza*. San Francisco: Spinsters/Aunt Lute.

Anzaldúa, G. (1988). Tlilli Tlappalli: The path of the red and black ink. In R. Simonson and S. Walker (Eds.), *Graywolf annual five: Multi-cultural literacy* (pp. 29–40). Saint Paul, MN: Graywolf.

Athayde, R. (1977). *Miss Margarida's way*. New York: Avon Books.

Au, K. (1980). Participation structure in a reading lesson with Hawaiian children: Analysis of a culturally appropriate instructional event. *Anthropology and Education Quarterly, 11*, 91–115.

Au, K., & Kawakami, A. (1991). Culture and ownership: Schooling of minority students. *Childhood Education, 67*, 280–284.

Au, K., & Mason, J. (1983). Cultural congruence in classroom participation structures: Achieving a balance of rights. *Discourse Processes, 6*, 145–167.

Augenbraum, H., & Stavans, I. (Eds.). (1993). *Growing up Latino: Memories and stories*. Boston: Houghton Mifflin Company.

Bao Lord, B. (1990). *Legacies: A Chinese mosaic*. New York: Alfred A. Knopf.

Bruner, J. (1987). Life as narrative. *Social Research, 54*, 11–32.

Candelaria, N. (1993). The day the Cisco Kid shot John Wayne. In H. Augenbraum and I. Stavans (Eds.), *Growing up Latino: Memories and stories* (pp. 115–130). Boston: Houghton Mifflin Company.

Carter, K. (1993). The place of story in the study of teaching and teacher education. *Educational Researcher, 22*, 2–12.

Cisneros, S. (1989). *The house on Mango Street*. New York: Vintage Books.

Delgado-Gaitan, C. (1990). *Literacy for empowerment*. Bristol, PA: Falmer.

Didion, J. (1994). On the morning after the sixties. In S. Cahill (Ed.), *Writing women's lives: An anthology of autobiographical narratives by twentieth-century American women writers* (pp. 251–254). New York: HarperCollins.

Duran, R. (1983). *Hispanics' education and background: Predictors of college achievement*. New York: College Entrance Examination Board.

Edelsky, C. (1986). *Writing in a bilingual program: Habia una vez*. Norwood, NJ: Ablex.

Eisner, E. (1988). Foreword. In F.M. Connelly and D.J. Clandinin, *Teachers as curriculum planners: Narratives of experience* (pp. ix–xi). New York: Teachers College Press.

Emerson, G.J. (1983). Navajo education. In A. Ortiz and W.C. Sturtevant (Eds.), *Handbook of the North American Indians*, Vol. 10, *Southwest* (pp. 659–671). Washington, DC : Smithsonian Institute.

Farr, M., & Daniels, H. (1986). *Language diversity and writing instruction*. New York: ERIC Clearinghouse on Urban Education.

Foster, L. and Foster, L. (1993). *Fielding's Mexico*. New York: William Morrow and Company.

Freire, P., & Macedo, D. (1987). *Literacy: Reading the word and the world*. South Hadley, MA: Bergin and Garvey.

Gibson, M. (1987). The school performance of immigrant minorities: A comparative view. *Anthropology and Education Quarterly, 18*, 262–275.

Greene, M. (1988). *The dialectic of freedom*. New York: Teachers College Press.

Griffin, J.L. (1988). Forging new schools: Innovations pay off elsewhere. In J.D. Squires (Ed.), *Chicago schools: The worst in America* (pp.159–167). Chicago: Chicago Tribune.

Heath, S. (1982). What no bedtime story means: Narrative skills at home and school. *Language in Society, 11*, 49–76.

Heath, S.B. (1983). *Ways with words*. Cambridge, UK: Cambridge University Press.

Heath, S.B. (1986). Sociocultural contexts of language development. In C. Cortes (Ed.), *Beyond language: Social and cultural factors in schooling language minority students* (pp. 143–186). Los Angeles: Evaluation, Dissemination, and Assessment Center, California State University.

Horan, A., & Thompson, D. (1985). *Mexico*. Amsterdam: Time Life Books.

Hughes, L. (1968). As I grew older. In A. Chapman (Ed.), *Black voices* (p. 426). New York: New American Library.

King, M., & Rentel, V. (1981). *How children learn to write: A longitudinal study* (Final report. NIE Grant G-79-0137 and G-79-0039). Columbus, OH: Ohio State University.

Kotlowitz, A. (1992). *There are no children here: The story of two boys growing up in the other America*. New York: Doubleday.

Lee, V. (1985). *1983–84 National assessment of educational progress reading proficiency Catholic schools results and national averages*. Washington, DC: National Catholic Educational Association.

Lobel, A. (1982). *Ming Lo moves the mountain*. New York: Greenwillow Books.

Mitchell, W.J.T. (1981). *On narrative*. Chicago: Chicago University Press.

Moll, L. (1992). Literacy research in community classrooms: A sociocultural approach. In B.R. Beach, J.L. Green, M.S. Kamil, and T. Shanahan (Eds.), *Multidisciplinary perspectives on literacy research* (pp. 211–244). Urbana, IL: National Council on Teachers of English.

Moll, L., & Diaz, S. (1987). Change as the goal of educational research. *Anthropology and Education Quarterly, 18*, 300–311.

Morgan, W.R. (1983). Learning and student life quality of public and private school youth. *Sociology of Education, 57*, 187–202.

Nieto, S. (1992). *Affirming diversity: The sociopolitical context of multicultural education*. New York: Longman.

O'Dell, S. (1960). *Island of the blue dolphins*. Boston: Houghton Mifflin.

Olson, D.R. (1990). Thinking about narrative. In B.K. Britton and A.D. Pellegrini (Eds.), *Narrative thought and narrative language* (pp. 99–112). Hillsdale, NJ: Erlbaum.

Pacyga, D.A., & Skerrett, E. (1986). *Chicago: City of neighborhoods*. Chicago: Loyola University Press.

Paulsen, G. (1978). *The night white deer died*. New York: Bantam Doubleday Dell Publishing Group, Inc.

Perez-Miller, A. (1991). *An analysis of the persistence/dropout behavior of Hispanic students in a Chicago public school*. Unpublished doctoral dissertation, University of Illinois, Chicago.

Phillips, S. (1983). *The invisible culture: Communities in classroom and community on the Warm Spring Indian Reservation*. New York: Longman.

Robles, J.J. (1988). One out of three is poor in Pilsen. *Chicago Reporter*, pp. 3, 8, 10.

Rodriguez, L. (1993). *Always running: La vida loca, gang days in L.A.* Willimantic, CT: Curbstone Press.

Rodriguez, R. (1982). *Hunger of memory: The education of Richard Rodriguez*. New York: Bantam Books.

Rodriguez, R. (1992). *Days of obligation*. New York: Viking.

Schubert, W.H. (1986). *Curriculum: Perspective, paradigm, and possibility*. New York: Macmillan.

Smith, B. (1981). Narrative version, narrative theories. In W.J.T. Mitchell (Ed.), *On narrative* (pp. 209–232). Chicago: University of Chicago Press.

Steinbeck, J. (1937). *Of mice and men*. New York: Covici-Friede.

Steinbeck, J. (1947). *The pearl*. New York: Viking-Penguin.

Trueba, H. (1989). *Raising silent voices: Educating the linguistic minorities for the 21st century*. New York: Newbury House.

U.S. Census Bureau. (1991, February). *U.S. Census of Chicago race and Latino statistics for census tracts, community areas and city wards*. Chicago: City of Chicago.

Valdés, G. (1982). *Puentes y fronteras: Coplas chicanas*. Los Angeles: Castle Lithograph.

Valdés, G. (1996). *Con respecto: Bridging the distances between culturally diverse families and schools: An ethnographic portrait*. New York: Teachers College Press.

Valdivieso, R. (1986). Hispanics and schools: a new perspective. *Educational Horizons, 64*, 190–197.

van Manen, M. (1991). *The tact of teaching: The meaning of pedagogical thoughtfulness*. New York: State University of New York Press.

Villaseñor, V. (1991). *Rain of gold*. New York: Laurel.

Walker, C. (1987). Hispanic achievement: Old views and new perspectives. In H. Trueba (Ed.), *Success or failure? Learning and the language minority student* (pp. 15–32). New York: Newbury House/Harper and Row.

Weisman, A., & Dusard, J. (1986). *La Frontera: The United States border with Mexico*. New York: Harcourt Brace Jovanovich.

Wong-Fillmore, L. (1986). Equity or excellence? *Language Arts, 63*, 474–481.

Index

About the Author

Chris Liska Carger, Ph.D. is presently an assistant professor in the Department of Curriculum and Instruction at Northern Illinois University. She has worked with bilingual students in New York and Chicago for 20 years. She has also written numerous journal articles on multicultural education and the use of multicultural children's literature with second language learners.

Chris' doctoral work was completed at the University of Illinois at Chicago, where her dissertation, from which *Of Borders and Dreams* emanantes, was nominated for a Distinguished Dissertation Award.

DATE DUE

ILL			
7032367			
7/16/03			
OC 26 05			

#47-0108 Peel Off Pressure Sensitive